SPEAKING HIS MIND

STEPHEN JOEL TRACHTENBERG

AMERICAN COUNCIL
ON EDUCATION
Series on Higher Education
ORYX PRESS
1994

FOR FRANCINE, ADAM, AND BEN—

THREE WHO WERE NOT SURPRISED BY
THE TITLE OF THIS BOOK—

WITH LOVE AND GRATITUDE FOR THEIR
ENDURING ENCOURAGEMENT AND SUPPORT

CONTENTS

FOREWORD

Universities today find themselves in a paradoxical situation. Around the world, they are acclaimed as leaders in education, scientific discovery, and scholarly research. To the ablest students from abroad, the United States is the country of choice in which to pursue advanced study. In worldwide opinion surveys, American universities dominate the list of leading institutions of higher learning. In Stockholm every December, American university scientists take home a major share of the year's harvest of Nobel prizes.

Yet here at home, in vivid contrast, our colleges and universities are experiencing a markedly different reception. A series of widely read authors criticize their teaching, accuse them of political conformity, and attack their curricula and admissions policies. Government officials condemn their financial practices and bring suit against them for colluding in their student aid policies. National magazines carry annual complaints about their spiralling costs and out-sized tuitions. All in all, the atmosphere is far from what one might expect for institutions so widely admired abroad.

Clearly, there is something odd going on, some lack of understanding about how well universities are performing and what they can reasonably be expected to accomplish. Such misunderstandings are always unfortunate but particularly so today. For better or for worse, universities have become critical to the welfare of the nation, because they are our leading source of supply for three ingredients essential to the success of a modern society: new discoveries, expertise, and a highly educated people. It is precisely because universities are so important that their role in society is increasingly questioned, their activities scrutinized, and their shortcomings widely deplored.

In these times of criticism and confusion, university presidents become more important than ever, because they occupy such strategic ground from which to interpret their institutions to society and relay society's concerns back to the academy. No one else can so plausibly speak for the entire university community to the outside world. Nor can anyone else so readily harvest the concerns of parents, government officials, corporation executives, foundation heads, and other interested parties and explain to academic audiences what the public expects of universities and what it thinks it is getting.

It is unfortunate that at a time when their voices are most needed in public debate, university presidents are perforce heavily distracted with other pressing issues. It is no secret that higher education, like other major institutions in society, is going through a difficult time trying to make do with less by downsizing, restructuring, and otherwise coping with a chilly financial climate. Presidents need to raise huge amounts of money to maintain decaying buildings and offset declining appropriations and grants from government sources. Difficult cuts must be made, requiring endless meetings with administrators and faculty. At such times, books, articles, reports, and other communications to the outside world must often be sacrificed to demands of more urgent business at home. And so it is that one hears very little in response to the torrent of criticism that has fallen upon universities in recent years.

Under these circumstances, it is especially fortunate that Stephen Trachtenberg has chosen to publish a collection of his recent speeches on a wide variety of subjects important to higher education. More than most of his colleagues, he has managed to find time, not merely to speak but to devote unusual effort and thought to sharing his ideas about universities with an array of interested audiences. Better yet, he has unfailingly managed to do so with grace and wit, not to mention a fetching capacity to look upon himself, his work, and his institution as fit subjects for humor as well as sober reflection.

Very few of the recent controversies of higher education go unremarked in these pages. Readers may not agree with all of President Trachtenberg's ideas on these controversial topics. Even I would have a bone or two to pick along the way. But few people will come away from this book without a greater understanding of American universities and what they are trying to do to satisfy the legitimate demands of a critical public. —*Derek Bok*

Derek Bok is President Emeritus of Harvard University. Among his academic degrees is a Master of Arts earned at The George Washington University in 1958.

SPEAKING HIS MIND

1989

REASON AND HEART TOGETHER

There is a prayer which might have been custom-made for my use today. It reads: "You and I know, O Lord, that I do not merit these titles of honor. But, since so many good people believe them in all sincerity, I beseech Thee to aid me to avoid the snares of Satan, so that these people may not be disappointed."

It's rare for a person to be able to say to a large number of fellow human beings that they are witnessing him on the single most important day of his professional life, but I have no hesitation in saying it to you today. After a quarter-century or so of effort, starting with the day I received my law degree from Yale, I can look back upon all kinds of experiences, adventures and achievements, including a few triumphs. None of them, however, approaches the level of what I am experiencing today in terms of pride, pleasure, happiness and joy. If only my parents were here to enjoy this moment with us . . .

My feelings are all the more intense as a result of the nine months I have already experienced here at The George Washington University. I suppose we're all familiar with the moment when a brand-new officer stands up to deliver his or her very first speech. If the speaker has only been on the job for a couple of weeks, the audience is usually undecided as to whether the person they are listening to is a mountain-climber who is launching the organization toward new heights of accomplishment or an innocent lamb offering itself up for sacrifice. The new "leader" may be quite uncertain on that score as well.

Having been here for such an eventful gestation, however, I can tell you that I don't feel at all like a lamb. Nor, if truth be told, do I feel like a mountain-climber carrying The George Washington University in his backpack as he aims for the higher reaches of Annapurna or Everest. To find an adequate analogy for what I *do* feel, I'd have to switch from metaphors altogether and say that I am experiencing the sentiments, if not the actual physical size, of a jockey—one who knows in his bones that he has chosen the superb thoroughbred with whom victory is not a possibility but a likelihood . . . and best of all, who knows that when offered a paddockful of talented and ambitious jockeys the thoroughbred chose *him*.

When, 12 years ago, I was inaugurated as president of the University of Hartford, it would never have occurred to me to allow images from the world of horse-racing to enter my inaugural address. The year was 1977 rather than 1989. American universities were trying hard to adapt to the economics of inflation and the shift of undergraduate interest toward the world of business. But American universities, like the nation whose needs they were struggling to serve, had not yet confronted scenarios of such unlimited competitiveness as those that so often dominate our thinking today.

High school seniors trying to gain entrance to the schools that will do them the most good are competitive to an extent that bothers the schools themselves—because they don't see learning as something that necessarily thrives when battlefield psychology has taken it over.

The schools are competitive with each other to an extent that often bothers the American public—people who feel uneasy when marketing skills, formerly confined to the corporate sector of the economy, are used to sell higher education.

Nations, in turn, supported by their educational systems, are engaged in competition with each other that is fiercer than at any time since the Second World War—and are beginning to feel some uneasiness about the psychological, ecological and even medical consequences of an obviously interminable struggle between sovereign entities, each of which is trying to gain for its own citizens what won't be available to the citizens of other countries.

In the world of 1989, therefore, a university president needn't be quite so apologetic about using what was once called the "Sport of Kings" to describe the collective enterprise upon which he or she has, by definition, embarked. But a university president may be open to criticism if, having used the analogy, he or she simply leaves it at that. Which in turn explains why I'm going to devote the remainder of my address first to an assessment of GW's very competitive position in

American academic life, and then to the whole subject of competition and its relation to learning.

What my experiences at The George Washington University have taught me is that you and I are, in our various ways, affiliated with a school that can truly be thought of as an academic thoroughbred, groomed for precisely the challenges that face the United States and its higher education system right now.

Since the time when most of our present undergraduates first saw the light of day, somewhere between 1967 and 1971, the challenges we confront—be they demographic, or economic, or ecological—have become typically global. They now typically involve the central governments and capital cities of all of the nations involved. And they typically involve many more nations than might have been the case 10 or 15 years ago.

I don't need to expand at length, therefore, on the significance of The George Washington University's location, of its relationship to that location, and of the sustained tradition through which that relationship has evolved.

In your inauguration programs, most of you have already seen an account of the presidents this school has had from 1821 to 1989, narrated against the background of American history. Though the account definitely has its high points and not-so-high points, it does communicate the extent to which the fortunes of the University have been intertwined, in a most unusual fashion, with the fortunes of our federal government as it, in turn, has set policy for the nation as a whole. During the lifetimes of Andrew Jackson, John C. Calhoun, John Quincy Adams and Henry Clay, GW had already established itself as a major source of training for the civil servants, political figures and diplomats who actually ran the government. The years since the Civil War have seen that function steadily gain in significance as a priority mission of the school. That is why the University continues to draw so many students whose eyes are set on careers in national and international affairs.

The George Washington University's location facilitated its development into what George Washington himself thought of as a "national university." Equally important, however, was the wisdom of the faculty members, administrators and trustees who grasped that role with both hands and held onto it for a period of more than a century. And here we should not minimize the significance of the school's Baptist roots, as well as the fact that its earliest presidents came from such strongly religious backgrounds.

The major world religions—including Judaism, Christianity and Islam—have always put teaching alongside revelation at the core of their value systems. What those early administrators, working with their faculty colleagues, sought to achieve was a university that would serve national need—but would do so guided by the North Star of ethical and humane behavior. From the very start they rejected the notion of making this a sectarian school. From the very start they sought to place it at the service of a nation committed to the cause of humanity, a nation that they prayed would pursue self-interest up to a certain point—but not to the point at which self-interest was its *only pursuit*. From the start, therefore, they saw the function of deeply committed teaching as one that would distinguish this university, functioning in the most influential of all American cities.

One of the things that has impressed me most of all at George Washington is the extent to which that early commitment to teaching has continued and has strengthened itself right down to the present time. Studying the assessments made of the school by third parties, including publications that make a point of evaluating the most important universities in the United States, I have been struck by how often they refer to George Washington University faculty members as teacher-scholars who are *still accessible to their students*—even when they are engaged in significant, sometimes world-class research, and even at time when many Americans assume that universities don't necessarily encourage good instruction aimed at other than top-flight graduate students.

What I am suggesting is that the continuity and coherence of this school's sense of mission makes its age of 168 years a somewhat misleading figure. The universities of Bologna or Paris or Oxford can claim roots that extend back nearly a thousand years. But they have undergone repeated transformations that make those roots physical and geographical rather than spiritual. This university's century-and-a-half plus

18 years have been spent, in contrast, on a mission that remains one of its major purposes today.

I've talked about The George Washington University's location, and about the school's sustained efforts to be worthy of that location by making the best possible use of it. That, I hope, has helped you to see more clearly why I regard it as a force within American higher education that will grow more powerful with the years—one that justifies my comparison of it to a splendidly groomed thoroughbred—so prepared to do its best that I, as president alias jockey, am trying hard to keep up with its strengths and working even harder to make certain they get effectively used. Now let me change the tack of my inaugural address and consider the ways in which no competitive metaphor, in and of itself, can truly do justice to the mission on which this university, and all of those affiliated with it, are presently embarked.

The United States has often been described as a nation whose democratic ideals make it naturally competitive. It took the French Revolution of 1789 to create, for the French middle class, the competitive ideal they referred to as "careers open to talent." Thirteen years earlier, however, the American Revolution was fought by people who had long assumed that openness to talent—the willingness to tolerate and encourage competitive individuality—was the very essence of their social contract, a concept they subsequently embodied in the American Constitution.

And yet, the United States, like the European countries from which it drew so many of its citizens, was a nation that had developed its values out of two sets of ideals: a competitive tradition traceable to the values of ancient Greece, and an anti-competitive tradition traceable to the ideals repeatedly expressed in the Bible.

As classicists often remind us, our modern English word *agony* is based on the Greek word *agon*, meaning a struggle or contest. When we talk about the *protagonist* of an ancient Greek tragedy, therefore, we are using particularly appropriate language because virtually every aspect of Greek culture was touched by the competitive ideal. The hero of a tragedy or of a tragic epic like the *Iliad* was grappling with fate itself, struggling, like Oedipus or Achilles, to avoid his doom. The

Hellenic poet or artist or architect, in turn was wrestling with all the other poets and artists and architects who had ever come to Greek notice, trying to achieve a still more perfect perfection. And as the modern Olympics continue to testify, the Greek athlete was seeking the transcendent joy of personal victory—but within a culture that regarded second- and third-place winners as no better than losers, a culture that defined "good guys" as those who come in first.

The tradition that we see developing in the pages of the Bible, on the other hand, felt from the very start a certain distrust toward those too intent on winning, and a certain pleasure when those muscle-men or muscle-nations were thwarted by underdogs like Abraham or Moses or David or Daniel. The Bible has contributed to our collective sensibility a deep abiding concern with justice rather than victory, and a sense that a justice can often be achieved only by those who have given up the notion of personal or organizational triumph.

It would be possible, I think, to write a history of the United States or a history of American higher education in which the main theme would be the oscillation between these two ideals. As early as the year 1821, when this school was founded—a time when European universities were still surrounded with theological and class barriers intended to keep outsiders out—American institutions of higher learning were free to declare their belief that all citizens deserve the chance to develop their talents and to apply them to the common good as well as personal advancement. And down to the present moment, the United States is a nation haunted by the sense that it may be compromising its original commitment to liberty and justice for all rather than a selected few.

In recent years, we have been passing through a swing of the national and international pendulum in the direction of heightened competitiveness. Now we seem to be entering a time of necessary counterbalance in the opposite direction, when physical, psychological and spiritual considerations mandate an ethic of well-directed cooperation.

In an uneven but anxious manner, the nations of the world are trying to turn planetary well-being into a value that can even intrude on national sovereignty—if only individual nations can be convinced to relinquish bits of that sovereignty in the interest of common survival.

At the national level, each industrialized country is having to struggle toward a new balance between the process of industrial development and the preservation of what industrial development was originally meant to serve, namely the quality of our individual and collective lives. Gone is the day when those concerned with the quality of life were regarded as enemies of those seeking to give us more and better products with which to improve life. With something close to culture shock, we are beginning to realize that like fish in a pond *we are all in this together*.

Meanwhile, within the world of higher education, the long reign of disciplinary separation and specialization is giving way to a search, however inchoate, for the common ground linking technological achievement with humanistic concern, objectivity with ethics, analysis with synthesis, ends with means.

I have given you quite a number of reasons for my pride in serving as president of The George Washington University, but I have saved the most important reason for last. It is the fact that this school is on the way to becoming *the* national forum for a discussion of the difficult transitions this species must make if it is to survive in a forum its sensitivities can tolerate, and one of the national embodiments of what institutions look like when they are thinking confidently and comprehensively rather than anxiously and automatically. As our academic and administrative appointments increasingly confirm, we are a university whose goals are universal and embracing, not parochial and fragmented—which is why we can claim, with so much justice, to be preparing our students for the world of the 1990s when desperate needs will run neck-and-neck with brilliant accomplishments, and when human intelligence and empathy will somehow have to cope with human destructiveness and mutual rejection.

Let me sum up this inaugural address. In coming to The George Washington University, I feel that I have come to the very center of our nation's life, to the very center of my own life, and to what will become, much sooner than skeptics can possibly imagine, an even more vital center of American academic life. The thoroughbred will run a race of a somewhat different kind from those of earlier ages— a race toward the finish-line beyond which our full humanity can begin to blossom, and competition will never again be a fight to the death.

"The heart has its reasons," wrote the French philosopher Pascal, "that the reason does not know." What we are doing here, at a university located in the heart of Washington, is to reason toward the marriage Pascal could not imagine, the union that at long last draws reason and the heart together. I am very proud, indeed, to be inaugurated today as the servant of a university that serves the world in which all of us hope to live.

Martin Buber tells a tale about the Ba'al Shem Tov, founder of the Hasidic movement. It seems that when he encountered a major problem, he would got to a designated place in the forest. There he would deliberate, light a fire, pray to the Almighty, and his dilemma was quickly resolved. When his successor, the Maggid, faced a challenge, he followed a similar pattern but discovered he no longer knew how to light the fire; however, he could make the prayer and when he did so, what he needed was also done. In the next generation, Rabbi Leib would similarly enter the forest, but he could not recall either how to kindle the flame or how to make the prayer. He, therefore, said, "We do recall the right place, so let that be sufficient." And it was. In the fourth generation, Rabbi Israel in a troubling situation would simply stay at home, saying, "The fire we cannot light, the prayer we cannot make, the place in the woods we cannot recollect. All we can do is tell the story. Let that suffice." According to Dr. Buber, it did.

Professor Walter Kaufman observed that something is missing and must be added. He insists that we record what the *next* generation said. They asserted, "The fire we cannot light, the prayer we do not know, the place remains lost, the story we are still able to tell but, unfortunately, we no longer believe it."

It is up to us to rekindle the flame. It is up to us to recall the prayer. It is up to us to find the place. It is up to us to keep the faith—for our own sake and for the sake of the generations yet to come.

Thank you.

Libraries are the Foundation on Which Universities Stand

When I was asked to provide a title for this talk, I chose, as you know, "Libraries are the Foundation on which Universities Stand." A detached observer could be excused the conclusion that for a speaker with an alleged reputation for "humor," this wording was oddly traditional—indeed, almost hidebound and old-fashioned.

But humor has a back door as well as a front door . . . and in this case, I felt that librarians like yourselves, who are so involved with words of every conceivable kind, would enjoy my use of a really solid metaphor like foundations at a time when both libraries and universities are shaking and quaking as they attempt to gain control of the words generated by our "information society," which has made the phrase information overload as familiar as tuition rise, smoggy day, traffic jam, ham and cheese, and oil-rich Kuwait.

Those of us who had the good or bad fortune to be educated in an earlier and simpler world, when even wars were fought by people who could sometimes actually see each other, can recall the college or university library as a place studded with references to the Middle Ages. Since the monastic scriptorium was our shared emblem of bibliographic heroism . . . the place where an occasional Latin or Greek classic was recopied when the monks weren't busy with sermons and hagiographies . . . it was perfectly appropriate that the college or university library be designed in Gothic style, and that the books sit on oak shelves solid enough to outlast the Apocalypse.

Little did we dream back then that something called cybernetics, the brainchild of a fellow named Norbert Wiener, would eventually sweep those miniature cathedrals of learning into virtual obsolescence. If a novel and film like *The Name of the Rose* has recently reminded us just how precious and restricted and locked up books were in the medieval period, a visit even to the local public library reminds us how things have changed since the thirteenth century.

The very first shelf likely to be encountered in today's public library is the one on which the videocassettes are stacked and eagerly thumbed through by those searching for movies like *The Name of the Rose*. Not too far away will be all the electronic gadgets that allow the patron in search of information to read *The New York Times* as published in September of 1949, or to examine the holdings of the Reading Room at the British Museum. Meanwhile, even a casual browse through some recent texts on James Joyce or Homer or Shakespeare will make it clear that those not armed with the appropriate hardware and software had better not enter a dispute on the precise text of *Ulysses*, the likelihood that the *Iliad* was composed by three people or 33, and the exact use Shakespeare made, from the beginning to the end of his career, of the conjunctions *and* and *but*.

What we now call the electronic library is in the process of supplementing and possibly supplanting the one with Gothic arches. In place of the vigilant monk or assistant librarian watching the reader with an eagle eye to prevent pilfering or mutilation, there are now all kinds of magnetic sensors and hidden cameras that perform the same function. And in place of the legendary reference librarian who could excavate, in less than 10 minutes, exactly the Old Testament passage being sought by a patron, we have software that will perform the same task in less than 10 seconds.

I suppose I'm not the only one who sometimes wonders whether the result, especially as entire libraries of information become available on floppy disks, will not be the disappearance of libraries as we know them, closely followed by the universities that stand on top of their electronic foundations. Already there are those who tell us, from either an ecological or an economic point of view, what a Nirvana awaits us when no one has to leave home except those who still insist on outdoor exercise.

A university president, once one reaches that blissful state, will hold his or her meetings via teleconferencing, while teaching will take place through a variety of modems and screens. Asked by the face on the screen what he or she makes of some lively interchange between

Othello and Desdemona, the college sophomore will summon up on his or her PC every literary and pictorial reference to handkerchiefs and strawberries since the Stone Age, and give an answer so definitive that we will hear the greatest Shakespearean scholars of former times whirling like pinwheels in their graves. Meanwhile, the ghost of Gregor Mendel will appear—in electronic form, of course—to emphasize that if only bibliographies had been computerized by 1880, the human race could have saved itself all kinds of "peaposterous" (sic) stumbling with regard to the science of genetics.

If we do enter a glorious future of that particular kind—I was about to say a shining future, but enough of electromagnetic metaphors!— the cost-savings will be obvious. Universities can shut their doors, and donate their campuses to the federal government as convenient places to store all the floppy disks needed to keep track of Social Security or the loans outstanding at the nation's savings and loan associations. Libraries too can be put to good use as recreation centers for a growing number of senior citizens. Their ceilings are often high enough, after all, to accommodate even basketball and volleyball games, while the oak table they still tend to favor should prove perfect for chess, checkers and backgammon.

I jest, but not altogether. References to our information society tend to be accompanied, these days, by references to the decentralization of data that is now well within sight of our information technologies—and I use the plural form advisedly. Combine the TV monitor with the computer, the telephone, the printer and the fax machine —and as all of you know, the race to combine the momentous technologies is only starting to gain momentum, and the future shape of the world that you and I now take for granted is, well, not to be taken for granted!

That, as I see it, is why current discussions of the electronic library, though often conducted with a certain bravado, still have a partial or even fragmentary look to them. For example, the recent report of the American Library Association's Presidential Committee on Information Literacy, while suggesting that the growing electronic availability of information is breaking the hold of "the old pyramids of influence and control," had to take note in passing of the fact that "about one out of every four undergraduates spends no time in the library during a normal week, and 65 percent use the library four hours or less each week" . . . and this despite the fact that school libraries now offer such an array of electronic facilities aimed at making research infinitely quicker and more convenient than could have been imagined even 10 or 15 years ago.

What the report does not go on to mention is the fact that these rather dismal figures offer a marked contrast to the amount of time that the average American student spends each week in front of the home or dormitory television screen, assimilating data that is entirely visual and oral—images and spoken words that have been meticulously structured in order to influence the viewer's opinions and behaviors, often in ways that employ psychological know-how of the most advanced and therefore subliminal kind.

Indeed, what I would like to suggest to you today is that the true challenge our world is offering to both our universities and the libraries on which those universities stand is not solely the challenge of gaining control over our informational Big Bang . . . but more importantly, the challenge of direct rivalry. One version of that state of affairs was exemplified by the global brouhaha over room-temperature nuclear fusion, when who-knows-how-many millions of dollars were spent by researchers trying to catch up with a single press conference. Had those researchers not been able to use fax machines in the struggle to gain their balance, additional millions would no doubt be in the process of expenditure this very moment.

Or take a phenomenon that I repeatedly hear of from professors of history—how much class-time is expended in trying to catch up with what students are convinced is historically true because they "saw it somewhere" or "heard it somewhere." A teacher at the university where I served as president from 1977 to 1988, prior to accepting my current assignment at George Washington, once told me of an entire class of freshmen nodding vigorously when one of their number declared, in ringing tones, that Hitler "was Jewish."

In other words, a world exploding with information may be a world in which it is increasingly difficult to control even ordinary people by restricting their access to information . . . but it is also a world in which bad information, if it has been made available in an effective manner, can, in a variation of Gresham's Law, drive out good information. That, surely, is why we are all so concerned about what, in the political context, is euphemistically called negative campaigning.

And often there doesn't have to be a Machiavelli controlling this process. The fact that a set of images, or a set of ideas, has been attractively presented—with no hidden political purpose—may still serve to give those images and ideas powerful, longstanding, ongoing roots in the minds of those exposed to them. Historians may labor to give us a true picture of rural life in the nineteenth century, for example, but will they ever catch up with *Little House on the Prairie*, all of whose kids wore picturesque outfits that had recently undergone careful drycleaning?

What I would like to suggest to you, indeed, is that a quantitative increase in the availability of information, when it takes on Niagara proportions that have accelerated geometrically each time we take a fresh look at them, amounts to a qualitative redefinition, one that often leads to particular and widespread feelings of despair. As every political or social or scholarly "scandal" swiftly produces whole armies of mutually contradicting authorities and pseudo-authorities . . . as controversy-levels worthy of the Dead Sea Scrolls or particle physics are generated over the misbehaviors of a congressman or a biographical detail in the life of a Hollywood star . . . it becomes less and less surprising to hear the man or woman in the street conclude that "we'll never be sure of the real truth" or that "I just don't have the time or energy to keep up with it."

And what that amounts to, I fear, is a de facto redefinition of truth itself, and a paradoxical reinvigoration of myth. In order to demonstrate what I mean by that, I'd like to draw on an example familiar to all of you—one that's uncomfortably close to home. In a recent issue of *Academe*, the bulletin of the AAUP—an issue largely devoted, in fact, to the electronic library—there appeared an article on a subject with which you and I are all too familiar, the escalating cost and wildly escalating quantity if scholarly journals. The author observed:

"Many of the specialist journals have a high cost-per-reader ratio due to very small circulations (often as few as 200 or 300), and are therefore supported almost entirely by libraries. One scientific publisher is rumored to scan the marketplace for large numbers of rejected papers and then start a journal to accommodate them! While it is questionable that this practice will attract many first-rate papers, the journals do sell, and authors have an outlet for a previously rejected work. The chilling aspect of this both in terms of wise use of library resources and the filling of the scientific pipeline with materials of questionable worth lies in a comment by an editor of a prestigious physics journal: he observed that many of the articles he rejects for factual errors later appear in less rigorously edited journals with the errors uncorrected."

"The filling of the scientific pipeline with material of questionable worth," now there is a grim phrase if ever I heard one, especially if we broaden our perspective to include the social sciences, the humanities, medicine, law and other disciplines. And indeed, the passage I have just cited confirms what we learned long ago, that as the sheer volume of uninspired or actively misleading work fructifies and multiplies, the handful of journals that insist on maintaining their high standards acquire, for their editors, unhealthy levels of power and influence over entire fields of knowledge, including the ability to unfairly squelch contradictory or unwelcome opinions that do have merit and should be granted a hearing. Compared to all of that, the assumption that Hitler was of course Jewish looks *almost* harmless!

Have I come here today, therefore, to tell you that we are in the middle of an information disaster? Or have I come here today to tell you that we must struggle even harder and more courageously, you and I, if we are to make knowledge and truth available in a world that is moved by electronic information and that moves, therefore, at the speed of light?

Truthfully, I have come here today to make neither of those points my main point. Rather, what I hope I have succeeded in conveying is the fact that the information challenges now being confronted by universities and libraries can be summed up as a single enormous challenge—that of a culture changing before our eyes "into something rich and strange." That last phrase is from one of the most famous and exotic of Shakespeare's songs, and I have chosen it because of my earlier reference to the paradoxical regeneration of myth that is perhaps inevitable in a world of exploding truths, half-truths and deliberate falsifications.

We can see parallels to the process we are undergoing in the history of the Roman Empire, whose dedication to secular expediency helped to feed a variety of orientalizing religions that put their emphasis on mystery rather than clarity in the way that rationalism and deism, in the eighteenth-century Europe, gave way to the Gothic Revival, full-blown Romanticism and a newfound dedication to the irrational. . .and in the fact that those, in the 1920s, for whom nothing was sacred helped to pave the way for those, in the 1930s, whose visions of transcendence proved quite compatible with murder.

Myth is not always murderous. But because it does not obey rational rules, like those employed at libraries and universities, myth is always lambent and unexpected, and often rides triumphant over fragile, vulnerable, nuanced and never-wholly-satisfactory truth. Whatever you and I do in our future careers, therefore, however we go about fulfilling our professional responsibilities, let us make certain that truth, however complex, continues to be our guide, no matter how large and complex the bibliographies in which we must search for it.

1990

A CAUSE CALLED JUSTICE

This is a very special time in human history. Just as the United States was once a land in tumult over the denial of civil rights to its minority citizens, so our entire world is now being shaken as huge numbers of people demand the rights, as well as the material benefits, that they feel have been denied to them.

In thinking about Dr. Martin Luther King and in considering how best to honor him on this anniversary of his birth, I think we must give him credit for being one of those who inspired this global revolution of expectations. Dr. King stood up in the middle of the most segregated portion of the United States and challenged his fellow Americans to live up to their own Constitution. He demonstrated what a single unarmed, peace-loving human being could accomplish in a world that often looked, to him and his followers, like one enormous bully.

Having achieved so much, and having given his own life in the process, Dr. King took his place in the tradition of human freedom based on an equality of rights and responsibilities . . . and of mutual decency between human beings based on the capacity to understand and therefore to share their feelings.

Any attempt to put Dr. King's life into a purely political framework seems to me very misguided. Though countless political gains resulted from his career, he himself was appealing to something more ancient and more universal than even the United States Constitution: the recognition by each human being that inside the other person there is also a human soul with human feelings, a soul that can be deeply hurt, scarred or even destroyed by behavior that is indifferent or actually hostile.

We know that's true where infants and children are concerned, which is why we never cease to be shocked by anyone who willfully brutalizes a child. But I think we tend to underestimate how much pain we feel, even as adults, when we allow ourselves to contemplate the true amount of hurtfulness that's loose in our world, the quite incredible extent to which people are willing to scar each other's feelings and to contemplate, without helping to alleviate, each other's pain.

I don't have to give you too many examples of that. Totalling up what you and I learn each day from the news media, the movies and our personal observations, our own feelings—even if we haven't been victimized in any deliberate way—are either somewhat lacerated or totally numbed. I myself can't read the Metro Section of *The Washington Post* without feeling my innards wrench this way and that. I feel uneasy each time the bureaucratic language of national or international politics seems to suggest that a veil is being drawn across a panorama of human anguish. And at a time when we are witnessing a worldwide rise in anxiety, and a rise too in all kinds of racist thinking, I experience moments of heart-stopping concern as I see the re-emergence of insults and stereotypes that we once thought we had buried forever.

That's why the memory of Dr. Martin Luther King grows in importance with each passing year. Dr. King's roots were in the Bible, and his university was the modern world. He knew, among so many other things, that the cause called justice is also the cause called humanity, and that humanity in turn means each and every one of us. Which one of us, if he or she were miserable, deprived, hungry, in danger of death, or in deep psychological pain . . . which one of us could stand to be ignored by the others around us on the ground that we should have taken better care of ourselves and prepared for any future disaster? Or that we're simply members of the wrong group at the wrong time? Which one of us, ignored in such a way, would not feel that he or she was being transported into a nightmare past that included slavery, indifference to the suffering of human beings labelled inferior, and actual genocide?

As Dr. King knew all too well, that nightmare past is still with us today. I lives on like some malignant growth within the deepest recesses of the human soul. When stresses reach a certain level . . . when stress is as high as today, and is getting even higher . . . we watch with a tightening of the heart as the hurtfulness, the coarseness, the willingness to cause or tolerate or ignore the infliction of pain on other human beings eats away at the core of our own personal humanity. The fact that such feelings are being put into words raises the possibility, given the history of the past two centuries, that they will lead to deeds—or equally significant failures to act. Threatened by indifference and hostility, we run all too great a risk of becoming indifferent and hostile ourselves.

In today's world, even more than in Dr. King's, we know too much to be innocent. . .and at the same time, we feel too limited in our individual humanity to ever do anything truly effective, especially if it seeks to meet the needs of others. The scale of suffering is so vast. Our individual strengths and capacities are so limited. Shouldn't we be looking after ourselves first of all, our families second of all, our ethnic or class compatriots third of all and our nation last of all? Can we spend additional time and effort trying to deal with a bitterly competitive world in which billions of people are struggling to obtain personal riches, personal happiness, or, at the very least, a single satisfying meal?

Dr. King stood up in his America—one man, in one pulpit—and he changed a nation forever. Now we confront a whole planet's cries for justice, and somehow we must learn to be—all of us together—the Martin Luther Kings of the 1990s, who understand the suffering of others, whose suffering is itself understood, and who are capable of action as well as words.

THE SEARCH FOR PERSPECTIVE IN A DE-CONTROLLED WORLD

The subject I would like to address is that of the relationship between the humanities, the social sciences and the natural sciences, and their collective relationship to our society in general, as we approach the end of the twentieth century and the beginning of a new millennium. Let me begin by saying that the relationship between those three aspects of what are usually termed "the arts and sciences" posed few problems when I was an undergraduate. Back then, the humanities—meaning written texts from the Bible and Homer to Dostoevsky, Nietzsche and Freud—were what you had to study for at least two years, with separate one-semester courses devoted to music and the fine arts. The social and behavioral sciences were mostly optional parts of the undergraduate curriculum, and still regarded, in the later 1950s, as a little flaky and uncontrolled. The natural sciences, neatly divided into chemistry, physics, zoology, astronomy and geology, represented, for all but a handful of majors, two difficult electives that many students put off until their junior and senior years—and didn't much care for even then!

In that much simpler world—simple, at any rate, in comparison to the one we occupy today—few instructors teaching Introductory Humanities bothered to inform us that paintings, poems, statues, novels and works of music had ever been created in East Asia or West Africa or pre-Columbian America. That was something you could find out for yourself if you registered for the appropriate electives, like Oriental Humanities or Anthropology 101 or Art History.

In that much simpler world, no one yet imagined that a Nobel Prize-winning chemist could be someone who almost never enters a laboratory but does his work while closeted with a computer—I'm referring to Dr. Roald Hoffman of Cornell, with whom I graduated from Columbia in 1959. And it would have sounded like fantasy rather than science fiction if anyone had imagined theoretical astronomers who referred to the universe as made up of "mind stuff," as one major scientist was to do within just a few years.

Back then, some of the most dramatic experimental proofs of Einsteinian physics were unavailable. No one had yet flown an atomic clock several times around the earth in a high-speed jet, successfully demonstrating that when it landed it was milliseconds *behind* the synchronized control-clock that hadn't budged from its spot near the runway. No one had yet thought of exploiting a complete solar eclipse in order to show that starlight IS bent by the sun's gravitation on its way to earth. No one had yet nailed down, on an unshakable statistical basis, that one suicide, when reported in the newspaper, is followed by a wave or wavelet of others—this despite Emile Durkheim's pioneering work on suicide at the beginning of the twentieth century.

And in a world fixated on Thor Heyerdahl and his raft Kon-Tiki as he struggled to show that pre-Columbian societies had been influenced—or at least influenceable—by the cultures of Southeast Asia, no one paid much attention to such known cross-cultural phenomena as the Roman mirrors found in Chinese tombs of the Han Dynasty; the Greek-influenced Buddhist sculptures of the earliest centuries A.D.; the coconuts that found their way to northern Europe during the Middle Ages and were promptly mounted, as drinking-cups for royalty and nobility, in gold and silver holders; the statuette of Buddha found in a Viking tomb; the extraordinary Afro-Portuguese ivories of the fifteenth and sixteenth centuries; the Benin bronzes of West Africa that were collected by Europeans as early as the first quarter of the eighteenth century; or the African sculptures that so strongly influenced Picasso and other artists of the early twentieth century.

No, back then "humanities" meant works created in the West, the "social sciences" meant mostly behavioral psychology, and the "natural sciences" meant clearly separable disciplines whose interdepartmental aspects were only discussed, by appropriately qualified researchers, at the postgraduate level. Back then, moreover, it looked and felt as if these neat definitions would endure forever and ever.

In the years that have elapsed between then and now, how the world of knowledge has exploded in all directions! And how desperately we are now running, especially within our universities and four-year colleges, to catch up with the consequences of that intellectual Big Bang!

Meanwhile, how desperate and sometimes frenzied have become the voices which assure us that the net result of this explosion is an enormous "new ignorance" in which politicized college curricula are aimed—or flung—at students more likely to push a button on their audio-visual equipment than to crack a book or open anything as daunting as a major newspaper.

Indeed, I would go so far as to suggest to you that what we are seeing in the world of ideas—the world that includes not only academic life but high culture in general—is actual panic as the verities of the 1950s crumble before our eyes and former agreed-upon truths and obvious realities are flung open to a multitude of questions and challenges. Holding one's tongue is certainly not the problem—all tongues are wagging, all fingers are typing, all dailies, weeklies, monthlies and quarterlies are publishing, and all screens are glowing as the charges fly back and forth between every gender, ethnic group and ideological position.

Meanwhile, an increasingly bewildered general public, exposed to the actual development of medical and scientific research by scientists who hold press conferences for the media that hang on their latest revelations, tries to grasp how last month's good news about cancer or cholesterol or global warming can be entirely contradicted and reversed in a period of only a few weeks.

Concealment is no longer our problem. Revelation is. Only persons of paranoid disposition any longer imagine that all physicians, all lawyers or even all businessmen are capable of sinister conspiracies aimed at depriving and defrauding the human race. I deliberately except government from that list, because conspiracies at the top of the various national pyramids have been all too copiously and sometimes tragically documented. No, the problem today, at least for the general public, is how to tell the *bona fides* or experimental accuracy or sound reasoning of ONE authority over the second one who maintains a 180-degree opposite position, especially when they are both sporting white coats or thick glasses or degrees from Harvard, Yale, Stanford and The George Washington University!

And if panic isn't the appropriate response, what is?

Now being a university president is usually considered a rather conservative kind of job. I myself, for example, am virtually required to show up in my office wearing a dark two-piece or three-piece suit, a silk tie and recently polished shoes. Were I ever to diverge from that pattern—by showing up in a plaid shirt and sneakers, for example—I would be taken, at best, as demonstrating some sort of philosophical principle, and at worst as having lost my mind. Nor would GW's Board of Trustees be amused for more than a brief time if I took to answering all my official mail by hand, using a green magic-marker held in my fist.

However, where the subject I am addressing today is concerned, I am about to risk a rather radical suggestion, namely the hypothesis that in the second half of the twentieth century we have recast our sense of time, of space and of human culture in a way so incredibly dramatic that the gulf between a stone-age tribe and the America of 1950 is narrower than that between America of 1950 and America of the present day.

That's a mouthful just to say, much less to explain! So like all really tidy people, I'll begin by making a list, beginning with our sense of time.

Number One: Most of us, when we aren't doing work that we actually hate, no longer experience the type of boredom, which the French have always called *ennui*, that was so common among even young people in the 1950s—the sense of absolutely nothing to do, no one to get in touch with, nothing worth exploring—the sense of time as a burdensome oppression, with the slow ticking of a clock as the epitome of personal emptiness. The availability of so many distractions and data-sources in the world around us, often accessible at the push of a button, enables typical modern human beings who live in industrial societies to move instantaneously from one set of brand-new phenomena to another, to extend consciousness as far and as fast as electricity can reach, and to communicate—again, instantaneously—with other people who in 1950 would have been weeks or even months away from contact.

Number Two: The same developments have radically eroded our previous sense of space. Miles count for nothing in today's world unless your car breaks down. Transmissions from outer space can reach Vladivostok as quickly as they reach Washington, Los Angeles, Bangkok or Cairo. The words and the face of a president or other leader can be studied on a split-screen whose other half is running the live coverage of a riot that contradicts everything he or she is saying.

And Number Three: The net impact of all this has been, is, and will continue to be a reversal of certain cultural assumptions that we owe to the Renaissance . . . and the restoration of a sense of reality not entirely unlike the one that prevailed in Western Europe during the Middle Ages.

It was during the Renaissance and the immediately subsequent period, after all, that some of our most central assumptions received their classic formulation . . . the *visual* assumption, for example, that there is such a thing as perspective, and its laws are absolute . . . the *philosophical* assumption that time is divided into equal and unchangeable units . . . the *cartographical* assumption that our planet can be neatly divided, on a two-dimensional surface, into space that is divided into equal units of latitude and longitude . . . the *literary* assumption, resurrected from the ancient Greeks, that every coherent work of prose or poetry must have a clear beginning, middle and end . . . the *bibliographical* assumption that all human knowledge can be gathered in printed works that in turn can be physically stored in many separate places and made available to all of those with the ability to read . . . and the *bureaucratic* assumption, epitomized in the work of Richelieu and Linnaeus and Descartes, that every aspect of life, from government to education to the animal and vegetable species, can be divided up into hierarchically arranged departments.

Those who lived in the Middle Ages were certainly not ignorant where geometry was concerned—otherwise, how could they have built such enormous cathedrals, only a few of which fell down? They certainly applied geometry to religious experience—as Dante and Aquinas demonstrate to the dismay of many modern readers.

But it took the Renaissance and post-Renaissance periods to suggest that a neat, compartmentalized, ultimately geometrical vision could be applied to every aspect of human life, and that human control—over the environment, over what were then considered the lower classes, and over physical reality itself—could therefore be infinitely extended. Systems of classification developed at that time, and amounting to nothing less than a comprehensive world-vision, are still with us today.

Pyramids of every conceivable sort—and there's an influential geometrical shape if ever there was one!—have been and continue to be erected for every human purpose imaginable, from schools and business organizations to government, the arts, literature, science and the determination of who's Number One and who's Number 55 among plumbers, electricians, discus-throwers, universities, fast-food restaurants, developers of nuclear and biochemical warfare, and builders of Taj Mahals and Eiffel Towers out of toothpicks, matchbook-covers and Frisbees!

The world-view we have inherited from the post-Medieval period, in other words, is one in which compartments are neat, progressions are clear, processes predictable, and the universe under mental control, which in turn has furthered the long-term human project of getting in under our physical control as well.

Now, I would like to suggest that we have entered a time marked by *de*-control—a time in which the very instruments with which we seek to establish control interfere with whatever goal they, and we who manipulate them, are trying to attain.

The phenomenon that now confronts us is nothing less than a mega-version of the uncertainty principle that faced nuclear physicists earlier in the present century. Back then, you'll remember, a cloud-chamber was the only way of "seeing" a nuclear particle, and what you saw was only where it had been. Attempts to catch it "live" through the use of light were frustrated by the fact that light, in one of its two simultaneous aspects, consists of photons, and that these particles would knock the ones under observation out of their courses.

Something very similar is true of an assumption that in 1950 was so obvious that it was never even discussed: the assumption that government could of course produce certain desirable results by creating a "program" whose "officials" would spend the money required in a logical way determined by other "officials" who had previously engaged in a completely rational, objectively perfect process called "planning."

For example, people might well have observed back then, if the subject had been discussed at all, that America was in the process of developing peacetime nuclear power of a kind so perfectly controlled that it would provide a 100-percent safe source of cheap power for every man, woman and child in the United States. And weren't we protected from our enemies by a defense system so brilliantly monitored that it was 100-percent fail-safe? And wasn't a wonderfully effective pesticide like DDT the perfect solution to the problem of world hunger?

How much more scared, how much less certain, and how much less optimistic we all have become in the intervening years. Even as our world has speeded up, even as it has become so much more contracted and accessible, even as we have extended the eyes, ears and memories of our computerized control-systems from pole to pole and out into space, we have become less certain, less trusting, less hopeful, and less assured about anything except the immediate present in which—for who knows how long?—we live.

I'd sum up the result as a loss of perspective. The ever-changing realities that now swirl and leap and billow all around us are like the figures in a Medieval woodcut, that bear some obvious relationship to each other but aren't located in a perspectival landscape or cityscape. Jesus confronts Satan, Lazarus is raised from the dead, a saint is tortured, Daniel looks a lion in the eye, Moses confronts Pharoah—*in the middle of no place in particular*. Even the soaring interior of a cathedral—originally so full of painted "special effects" *in addition* to the stained-glass windows—was designed to disarm and disable the sense of a clear, assured stability in which even the tallest tree had its limits and measurement kept things more or less under control.

Loss of control is what we are living with in the 1990s. Attempts to regain control seem like the obvious solution—the one we have inherited from our progenitors. But those attempts increasingly fail, or raise new problems of control that are even more mind-boggling.

Indeed, the most significant event of recent years, the one most laden with symbolism, may be the failure of the 1990 U.S. Census. With so much high tech at its disposal, so many new tricks for gathering and storing an infinity of data, the government of the United States could not count, to a minimally adequate extent, the population it represents. Measurement itself broke down—and measurement, more than anything else, is fundamental to the very notion of achieving control.

Having said all of these things—some of them rather grim!—let me end on a hopeful note. The new members of this Alpha Chapter represent a generation of Americans who will somehow have to deal with our new reality in new and right now unforeseeable ways. It will be your generational task to reconsider the very bases of our culture, our government, and our everyday philosophical assumptions—the ones that help to determine what we are capable of thinking and therefore are capable of doing.

We may live in a post-Renaissance world, but we also live in a pre-Something-Else world. And when we discover what the Something Else will look like and feel like, I have no doubt we will think back to you and your work and will say: "*They* brought us through. What felt at the time like collapse turned out, after all, to be creation. To *them* we owe the fact that we are no longer anxious or panicky but settled in our new way of life, with which we are reasonably but finally content."

1991

THE SEARCH FOR A NEW ORDER FOR PEACE, SECURITY AND COOPERATION IN NORTHEAST ASIA: LOOKING TOWARD THE 21ST CENTURY

Over the last several months, I have had numerous conversations and correspondences with Kyung Hee University's Chancellor Choue about the possibility of arranging an exchange program between our two schools—the possibility of becoming "sister" universities and providing our students with opportunities to immerse themselves in one another's culture and language. Today I want to talk about precisely what such programs can achieve. About the role of education in fostering global understanding. About the importance of having personal knowledge of people and places around the world. About what it is to know how people live and talk and think outside your country's borders. And about the power of travel in this day and age when telephones, fax machines, computers and an international news media reporting world events to our doorsteps and living rooms can appear to make it unnecessary to leave even your own home.

There has been a great amount of talk in recent months about a new world order. Our president, Mr. Bush, has invoked the concept regularly in discussing the recent events in the Persian Gulf. And we are all to search for "a new order for peace, security and cooperation in Northeast Asia."

On the international stage, the words "new world order" are akin in the possibilities they promise and the hopes they embody to two Russian words that the world has come to know well in recent years: *glasnost* and *perestroika*.

They are words brimming with promise and hope. Their power is that, in whatever language, they move us continually toward a utopian vision of our society and our world. Conversely, their fatal flaw, or perhaps ours in using them, is that we can raise our expectations to implacable levels while discounting the steadfastness of the various inertia we confront.

As such, these are words to be used responsibly and only if backed by concrete measures pushing us towards their fruition. Just as *glasnost* and *perestroika* still await a full definition in the Soviet Union, the events in the Persian Gulf awake us to the fact that a new world order does not happen overnight.

In looking at the state of global politics today, one recalls the oft-quoted opening of Charles Dickens's *A Tale of Two Cities*: "It was the best of times, it was the worst of times." On a baser level, one also recalls the way Americans introduce certain jokes with the line: "I've got some good news and some bad news."

Well, first the good news. An international coalition of nations led by the United Nations comes together to repel aggression by a man and an army considered a common threat to world peace. Our cooperation was unprecedented and its message to potential aggressors everywhere unforgettable.

And now the bad news. Despite this global show of unity and cooperation, we face a world gravitating more and more toward Balkanization. Increasingly, people and nations are dividing themselves from one another based on their sectarian, ethnic and nationalistic identifications. In today's world, the only government, the only spokespeople and the only compatriots worth anything are those aligned with us by race or religion or heritage.

Everywhere you look, it is one group against the other. The Serbs against the Croats in Yugoslavia. The Arabs against the Israelis in the Middle East. The Armenians against the Azerbaijanis in the Soviet Union. Even in seemingly peaceful countries like the United States, racial and religious and cultural tensions keep us from becoming truly one nation, one people.

It is in the face of this stubborn tendency toward separatism, isolationism and distrust that we must define common goals and work toward them together. While by all means we should celebrate those things that make us different, we must not neglect the things we share. Just as we worked together against a common enemy in the Persian Gulf, we must work together to stop other dangers that threaten us all.

A cursory look at world news of recent weeks and months reveals a preponderance of disasters and pestilence—events that seem beyond our control. There was the deadly cyclone in Bangladesh where more than 125,000 people died and millions are homeless; drought and famine in the Sudan and Ethiopia and other African countries with more than 35 million people at risk, according to the United Nations; cholera in Peru that is now spreading across South America; earthquakes in Soviet Georgia and Costa Rica and tornadoes in the United States.

According to a recent *New York Times* article, relief agency officials agree "that there has never been a time in recent history when so many disasters with such different natures have struck so many people."

We are reminded by these disasters of the commonality of our existence—of the fact that there are two things that we all truly share, and they are life and this planet we live it on. Disasters of the sort noted have no one nation or race or people as their targets. They are an indiscriminate enemy, they target us all, and they demand that we come to one another's aid.

They demand that we work together to protect ourselves and our fellow human beings from the whims of fate and nature. They demand that we remain focused on their potential to occur again—that we not forget their lessons once the television cameras turn away to the next disaster or disease or scandal. They demand that we remain attentive to things we can prevent, or hopefully temper, and in so doing protect ourselves from the anguish and the expense that come hand-in-hand in their wake. In short, they demand that we study, that we learn and that we educate.

It is easy to become numbed by the barrage of calamity and misfortune and sorrow that we are facing. It is easy to do as a New York City housewife recently told *The New York Times* she does. "I get upset watching the babies dying," she remarked. "Who the hell wants to see that? I switched the channel. There's so much going on at once."

What will keep us from doing likewise and switching the channel on an international scale, I believe, is more of an association with the world—more of a link between the citizens of individual nations and more understanding of global geography and cultures and languages. For if we have been somewhere, or if we know someone who has been there, and if that somewhere is suddenly in the news, it is only natural that we feel and understand more directly the impact of the events described. And it is only natural that we act.

Natural disasters and disease are not the only world events demanding our attention and action. We are threatened universally by the potential of man-made disasters caused by our continuing assault on our natural environment. It was the Chernobyl incident that sealed in all of our minds the fact that environmental problems, like natural disasters and disease, have no respect for international borders and boundaries.

Today we confront the global environmental impacts of rainforest destruction depleting our atmosphere of its capability to cleanse and cool itself; of man-made chemicals depleting the ozone layer and rendering us all potential victims of dangerous ultraviolet sunlight and of acid rain depositing pollution hundreds of miles away from its source and killing entire lakes and streams and even forests.

It could be that these environmental threats will have more to do with begetting a new world order than any aggression or war. They are problems whose impacts are demonstrable to all nations of the world. They are problems that demand timely solutions and significant behavioral changes among all nations. And they are problems we agree, for the most part, *are problems*, which is a significant first step to working together to solve them.

And the truth is that we *are* working together. The Montreal Protocol is one example of how the nations of the world can come together peacefully against a common threat—in that case the continued destruction of the ozone layer by man-made chemicals called CFCs. It is a model that should be replicated as we look at the other threats around us.

Critical among these other threats, and perhaps as dangerous as any noted here, is an issue of great concern in Northeast Asia.

The proliferation of weapons of mass destruction is an intolerable eventuality in a world striving for peace. Its persistence as a threat to peace shows precisely how far we have yet to go to reach our new world order.

That new world order demands that nations of the world open up their borders to scrutiny from the outside. Whether they are building nuclear weapons, spewing toxins into their air and water, or not cracking down on the spread of disease, they must be schooled in, and held accountable for, the global impacts of their actions.

It is an education, frankly, that I feel we all could use. For it is not only the more covert among us who put humanity at risk. We are all builders and buyers of weapons, all polluters of the earth. And we can all benefit greatly through the open exchange of the knowledge, the information, the technology and the people that can help us amend.

Today, approximately 400,000 students from around the world are studying at schools in the United States. That number is up from 311,000 in 1980 and 342,000 in 1985. At The George Washington University, we enrolled more than 2,600 students from 132 different nations last fall. That includes 275 from the Republic of Korea, 112 from China and 30 from the Soviet Union.

In fact, international students represent nearly 10 percent of George Washington University undergraduates and more than 16 percent of our graduate students. We are particularly proud that we rank fourth among U.S. universities in terms of the percentage of international students within the total student body, and fifteenth in terms of total international student enrollment.

Universities like George Washington, I would argue, are the only true multi-national melting pots on earth. They are places where students from around the world—potentially even from warring nations—gather in the same classrooms to hear the same professors give the same lectures. They are places where these same students have the opportunity to interact, to share insights, experiences and opinions about issues of the day. They are places, we hope, where citizens of different countries and cultures, including our own, come to understand and enlighten others.

International graduates of these universities are destined to return to their countries with newfound knowledge and understanding—and not just within their particular courses of study. They are destined to know more about the United States and other countries and to have personal knowledge of, and friendships with, individuals from around the world. On their return to their countries, they are destined to share this knowledge with their friends and their families and their colleagues at work.

By fostering such experiences—such global transfers of knowledge and understanding—I feel we can do no wrong. It can only be healthy for the nations of the world to have a greater knowledge within their borders of what lies without. The alternative, ignorance, is perhaps the most significant threat we face in the quest for peace and global cooperation. Because it is ignorance and the isolation it represents that ensure the survival of tyranny and oppression and general misconduct, whether it is in the area of environmental pollution or human rights violations. Exposed to the outside world, such things are like a fish out of water. They cannot live.

In fact, if one looks at the reasons for the fall over the last two years of Communist regimes in Eastern Europe, a common thread is clearly evident. More than anything else, it was an increasing awareness of the outside world that led the people of these nations to challenge their authoritarian leaders and to press for new freedoms.

In this day of CNN and global telecommunications and instantaneous satellite transmissions, it is hard for a country to hide any repressive or aggressive aims. Equally hard are efforts to shelter an entire citizenry from free-wheeling influences at play in other regions of the world. I would argue, in fact, that the fall of Communist regimes in Eastern Europe is a precursor to similar openings in Northeast Asia. As Communist and closed-door cultures become more and more isolated, their citizens more and more restive for the kind of change they understand is under way beyond their borders, the doors will open to freedom and international cooperation. It will take time and perhaps great struggle, but it is inevitable.

And the role of education in enabling us to nurture and take full advantage of these openings cannot be overemphasized. A recent poll of adults in Czechoslavakia, Hungary and Poland by the American Jewish Congress reveals that the mere lifting of an Iron Curtain does not guarantee meaningful change. Two out of three persons questioned in these countries said democracy is facing serious problems. A majority have little or no confidence in free-market initiatives their governments have undertaken.

As these and other nations seek to re-enter the global family, it remains critical that we provide them with the wherewithal to rebuild and to compete in a global economy. We must provide them with insights into our forms of government, our marketplaces and the special challenges we face in upholding individual freedoms and democracy. In short, we must provide them with a readiness that will preclude their retreat to antiquated and counterproductive ways.

What we also must provide—and we must provide it broadly—is less technical. It is the knowledge and understanding of different cultures and different people that, as I have mentioned, come through international education and exchange.

There has been a great deal of discussion in the United States recently about the extent to which we should indoctrinate students in a uni-cultural course of study—to teach the origins and implications of Western civilization at the expense of our society's multi-cultural heritage.

One argument says that our society draws its unique dynamism from its diversity—from the interweaving of countless cultures and perspectives. The teaching of Western ideas, the argument goes, aims only to subvert our cultural differences and to deny people of their most basic freedoms to associate and to express themselves.

The other argument is as follows: We live in a freely elected, democratic and free-market society founded on centuries of Western thought. Thus a full grounding in our society's origins is necessary if we are to remain faithful to the principles that fuel its government and institutions.

I am partial to this second argument. On the international stage especially, it is my belief that for an American, a grounding in American and Western civilizations is of critical value. Because the greatest value that American society offers to others around the world is as a model for the democratization of government, the protection of individual rights and the privatization of commerce. It is not a flawless model, of course, but it is a longstanding one and one that is constantly being tested for its faithfulness to democratic and free-market principles.

Americans who have no such grounding, I fear, offer little to other nations seeking to measure their progress toward freedom. Similarly, Americans who cannot speak English or who do not have the necessary technical background are of little value to nations craving needed assistance in understanding, and in benefiting from, our language and culture.

The situation is the same all the way around the world. Every nation has something to offer, and that something is itself—its own language, its own cultural identity, its home-grown technical expertise. In other words, we are all of value to one another for the different perspectives we bring to solving critical global problems.

We are all of value, that is, if we know our own cultures well enough to be able to provide others with some of the same knowledge. And to provide others with that knowledge, of course, we must also be able to communicate, to speak foreign languages and to understand questions and reactions we receive based on an understanding of other cultures.

There's a lot to understand, a lot to know, a lot to teach these days. Not to mention a lot of people to teach it to. American author Joseph N. Pelton figures that in the next 30 years there will be a need to educate more people than all of the people educated since the beginning of civilization—more than six billion individuals.

What will it take to teach this onslaught? In the face of such numbers, how can we build understanding and knowledge to the point that we are equipped to help power a global economy and to help keep peace? What does it take to educate six billion youths in the intricacies of our own cultures and our own languages and simultaneously in the ways and the words of other nations?

Like everything else, it takes a commitment. It takes a commitment to directing our resources to providing educational opportunity. It takes a study of how we view education—whether we see it, as we should, as an investment in our economies, our defense and our common future. Or whether we view it the old way—as a line item in a budget for domestic programs, a sacrificial lamb for other priorities of the day.

In the United States, with the Cold War cooling further into oblivion, there has been talk of a peace dividend—a surplus of government monies that would be infused into domestic and other programs as a result of the waning need to sustain a mammoth defense capability. In the face of billion-dollar deficits, however, this dividend has not revealed itself. And the recent events in the Persian Gulf have sealed in the minds of Americans and others around the world the continuing need for a powerhouse army on the global scene, if only as a symbol and a reminder that aggression will not be tolerated.

But can we not spend less on our armies and keep them adequate, even make them better? The United States, for example, is engaged in a comprehensive review of how the current structure of our armed forces meets current needs. The defenses we have in place were built for a Cold War during which we prepared to go to battle against another superpower. That is no longer the case. As the Persian Gulf War has shown us, today's defenses must be more compact, more mobile and based more on short-range and conventional capabilities.

Specifically, the success of high-technology weapons in the Persian Gulf War revealed to us that mass does not necessarily an army make. By equipping ourselves with the necessary technology, backed by appropriate troop strength, we can credibly defend our borders and deter aggression while decreasing our reliance on huge forces and expensive long-range systems.

In fact, while I do not profess to be an expert of any sort on military affairs, I nonetheless cannot help but think that it is the huge forces and long-range capabilities of certain nations that compromise opportunities for peace. We are threatened so by another country's build-up that we initiate or continue our own—until the world is weighed down with armaments and troops and with governments looking to justify their expenditures.

So where would we spend the money we save from streamlining and updating our armed forces? On education, of course. In fact, I would propose that if our governments were to spend on defense what we all currently spend on education, and on education what we now lay out for defense, our armed forces and our educational systems would both improve. And both would be significantly more responsive to the realities of the modern world.

And internationally, we must support opportunities for educational exchange. As we commemorate the tenth anniversary of the United Nations International Day of Peace, we must call on our governments, together with the United Nations, to foster international scholarship programs. In all of our countries, student leaders should be encouraged—no, prodded—to spend a portion of their academic careers abroad, traveling and studying the cultures and the languages of other nations.

For it is travel and direct experience and understanding that demystify the world. From our living rooms and dens, the world can seem a large and untenable and unwieldy place. In the news we watch and read, it is a place populated with radicals and riots. With masses of people that are either incensed or distressed. With misfortune and anger that can be so intense that we are daunted from even trying to understand their causes.

Lost in the media's translation is the fact that it is a world of individuals like ourselves—curious and inquisitive and always striving to improve their lot. They are individuals from whom we can learn many things. And in meeting and knowing them we take hold of the world—and we come to understand more precisely the true meaning of peace and a new world order.

THE ROLE OF BUSINESS IN EDUCATION

Gulliver's Travels, published in 1726, has taken on new meaning as a metaphor to describe the situation of the United States in 1991. Here we are, living in a country that once struck the world as the very embodiment of dynamism and movement as it extended its influence across the North American continent and all of Planet Earth, forged an unprecedented multitude of ethnicities and nationalities into a political engine of ceaseless, ever-innovating change and experimentation and looked, to foreign observers, like a nearly infallible preview of the future that would soon confront our species.

And now we can be forgiven if we rub our eyes in wonderment as we contemplate how things seem to have changed. Gulliver lies bound in a thousand knots and a hundred self-contradictions, dilemmas and conflicts. Bitter battles between ethnic groups, genders, life-styles, classes, religions and all of those seeking a bigger slice of diminishing budgetary pies—federal, state and municipal—are now the order of the day.

And in some strange way, America's schools of higher education have come to embody Gulliver's dilemma as they seem hopelessly entangled in debate over political correctness—the ubiquitous "p.c."—curricular content, Western Civilization and the Western humanities versus multiculturalism and diversity, research versus teaching, affirmative action versus free and open competition in the quest for achievement, et cetera et cetera *ad infinitum* and, quite frequently, *ad nauseam* too!

The long and the short of it: Gulliver, whose stride was once continental and indeed planetary, just *lies* there, unable to stand up. The sarcasms of foreign observers become all too familiar. The long-standing Japanese put-down—that "Japan is a factory, America is a farm, and Europe is a boutique"—seems to need modification only where Europe is concerned.

However, one recalls the Gettysburg Address and wonders whether a country put together the way ours presently is—caught in the grip of adversary thinking that claims to be the apotheosis of democracy—can long endure.

There is indeed some evidence of a new *world* order, including the *possibility* of reconciliations among previously adversarial nations. But, can we even begin to imagine a reconciliation for *ourselves*—for the increasingly *Dis*united States of America? A reconciliation large enough and pervasive enough to get Gulliver back on his feet again, showing the world what he can do when he's no longer paralyzed?

To me, one thing seems certain. Gulliver—meaning America, obviously—is not going to do that without a big and unified boost from two parties who don't always see eye to eye. One of them is Education. The other one is Business.

It seems like only the day before yesterday that they seemed to be, in some way, archetypal opposites—that truly self-respecting undergraduates opted for anything *except* a career in business. It seems like only yesterday that we swung in exactly the opposite direction—with the MBA degree trouncing all of its academic competitors, while university development officers wore out the carpeting in the hallways that lead to the executive suite of our major corporations.

And it feels like today—like *right now*—that those same executives are lamenting the extent to which they've been let down by American educators at every level from kindergarten to graduate school, the extent to which they can no longer take for granted that possession of an undergraduate or graduate degree means *anything at all* in terms of actual knowledge gained and usable skills acquired.

This in a country, moreover, where education has always played a more significant role than in any of the other industrialized democracies—precisely because our population is so incredibly diverse. And, this in a country where, for better or worse, from the time of Alexis de Tocqueville to our own age, *business* values have always been synonymous with *American* values—meaning the values most Americans take seriously.

What I've noted so far about the zigs and zags in the relationship between business and higher education has been implicitly focused on curricular issues—*what* gets taught and *how* it gets taught. There's another perspective now readily available on the relationship between business and education—one that underlies the extent to which they are *already* in a potentially cooperative rather than adversarial position. And this perspective is based on the concept of *efficiency*.

Back in the not-so-good old days, when those working in higher education felt about business the way folks in a horror movie do about the neighborhood vampire, one of their critiques had to do with the fact that business people were so grossly motivated by nothing but efficiency—also known as the quest for profits. But in the process of turning business into a bugaboo, those working in higher education were also able to elevate *inefficiency* into a positive virtue.

That attitude was centered on the old humanistic curriculum, with its shameless focus on European culture and its idealization of an academic style that *supposedly* prevailed at Oxford and Cambridge. What higher education ought to be, this particular vision declared, was an earthly paradise in which gentlemen of high intelligence gathered together to freely explore matters of the mind—relieved of financial anxiety, provided with excellent resources in the way of classrooms and libraries and protected from any nasty outside inquiries into what they were teaching and learning.

From today's perspective, we'd be forgiven if we said that this vision of an elite way of life—enthusiastically propagated at the very moment when American higher education was becoming a form of mass education—this elite form of life had a secret sponsor, very much like the character in Charles Dickens's *Great Expectations*. For higher education, the secret sponsor was none other than the despised world of American business, earning money hand over fist in order, among other things, to keep this academic paradise going and growing.

So American higher education became one of the very few enclaves in world history of which it could be said that the people in it were able to do *whatever they wanted*. Even Russian czars had to take account, after all, of the possibilities known as the block, the guillotine and the enraged mob. Only in American higher education did the money continue to flow no matter what you did, *no matter what you taught and no matter how you taught it or learned it.*

That became pretty obvious in the sixties. And it didn't end when Vietnam moved into the past tense. Universities and colleges, flying the banner of academic freedom, continued to be places largely defined by the teachers on their campuses, not the students. "Business-like efficiency" continued to be a no-no, even as the waters of the national economy turned cooler, then colder, then icy. And in a particularly insidious development, the administrative side of many universities and colleges learned to ape the academic side when it came to looseness of structure and a lack of interest in the relationship between money spent and practical results obtained.

Higher education sowed the wind of cheerful inefficiency. Today it is reaping the whirlwind of growing public distrust and disgust, of fiscal crisis and of Gulliver-like paralysis. Freedom to debate, freedom to move in any direction mandated by one's inner life, has led to endless and fruitless brouhahas over political issues sometimes only distantly—if at all—connected to actual learning.

The matter is well summed up by the issue of *The Chronicle of Higher Education*, dated November 20, 1991. The front page is dominated by a lead article on the sheer extent to which the financial roof has caved in on American higher education. Among other things, it points out that more and more students will be obliged to attend two-year rather than four-year colleges.

The house known as American higher education is burning down. And meanwhile, ream after ream of what gets paraded in front of our noses is taken up with the question of whether the fire engines have a proper coat of paint and are flawlessly registered with the bureaucracy.

Well, I've been a senior university administrator of long standing, and I say: enough with accreditation! Enough with disputes over curriculum! Enough with the polemics that are choking up American higher education's tubes, valves, gaskets and drains—or, if you prefer the metaphor with which I began, that's keeping Gulliver earthbound and helplessly thrashing.

The issue, right now, is whether we can provide the American people with the qualities and quantities of higher education that *they* need in order to make places for themselves in our national economy, and that it needs in order to hold its own against a lot—and a grow-ing amount—of international competition.

Does that mean I'm advocating a curriculum made up entirely of courses in applied subjects and crowned by an MBA? Absolutely not! That's fifties or sixties thinking applied to our nineties world, when the main skills demanded for business survival and advancement any-where on our planet are depth and breadth of knowledge, the ability to learn—if need be, quickly; if need be, thoroughly—and the abil-ity to adapt. More specific types of knowledge will be no problem to pick up, on the job if necessary, once these skills are in place. And among the subjects taught in a modern college or university that pro-vide these truly important skills are those taught in departments of English, history, foreign languages, art history, anthropology, psychol-ogy, religion and philosophy.

Let me sum up my thesis with a two-point program:

Step Number One: Throw the polemical garbage out the win-dow, where it belongs. In what the Marxists, when they were still around, called "objective" terms, debates of this kind now rank as acts of self-indulgence committed by America's economic and leisure elite—and as genuine abuses flung at the struggling heads of our needi-est citizens, many of them from minority groups. What *they* need and what we all need and what their *children* need and all our children need is education that leads to jobs, and jobs that lead to national economic renewal and to full lives for them and for America—lives that allow roles as family members, lives that allow jobs that pay a living compensation, lives that encourage civic participation.

Step Number Two: Get the academic and the business leaders together to determine (a) what schools of higher education must now do in order to achieve fiscal stability, and (b) how to accomplish that in ways that also serve the national economic interest.

And as for accreditation—meaning whether or not our schools of higher education are doing what they're *supposed* to be doing in order to meet federal standards for financial support—I'm prepared to con-tract measuring that to whatever bidder will do a good job for a rea-sonable amount of money . . . and if the Commission on Higher Educa-tion of the Middle States Association of Colleges and Schools would like to be among those bidders, there's no reason why then it shouldn't be considered. Surely those who care about the current association will continue to do so, even if it has no federal mission. The federal government can get what it needs and institutions of higher education can have what they want. We don't need a reluctant Department of Education to help us do what we believe is right to do. I know right from wrong without instruction or blessing from Uncle Sam.

An ethic of *inefficiency*, such as was developed by American higher education in the postwar "boom" years of the American economy, *did* help to determine curricular content. An ethic of efficiency does nothing of the sort.

Contained in our college and university curricula—in the sixties, seventies and eighties—was, to an ever-increasing extent, whatever interested those in charge of teaching them. And only the present "closing in" of the higher education economy, by demanding that *choices* be made—choices acceptable not only to intellectual critics but to the American public and its political representatives—has begun to force some coherence upon the resulting self-indulgent hodge-podge, already a front-page and prime-time issue exploited by our scandal-hungry media.

What gets taught from here on in, and how it gets taught, will have to meet so-called academic "marketplace" considerations. But what the marketplace is demanding right now is education that serves economic and cultural viability on an international basis, with all of the breadth and depth and intellectual *savoir faire* that standard implies.

And now is the time for American business to play *its* role—at a moment in academic as well as national history when change, reform and major improvement are at last a real possibility.

First comes role modeling. American corporations need to become more efficient themselves—without defining efficiency as callousness and cruelty.

Second comes recognition. Like it or not, American businesses *need* American higher education—and that's going to become truer and truer as the American work force comes to consist, to an ever-widening extent, of citizens from minority groups, of citizens who are recent immigrants to these shores, and of citizens who need a *lot* of support in tuning themselves to the needs of this world's profoundly competitive, utterly interdependent and increasingly international economy. We're talking about a work force that's going to have to go up against and/or work with the finest products of the University of Tokyo, of the University of Seoul, of Oxford and Cambridge, of the University of Berlin and of other world-class schools.

And third comes intelligent cooperation. If American higher education is not to become *just* a political football, subject of election-year sarcasms and media exposés, then American business must play the role of mediator. Among other things, America's corporate leaders must serve as guarantors to the American public of the fact that higher education has got its spending practices into reasonable alignment with its productivity—and that it is producing the kinds of graduates (and research) who (and which) bolster rather than erode the status of the American economy and the viability of individual wallets, pocketbooks and household budgets.

Will business have to continue playing a developmental role as well? In other words, will our corporations have to contribute actual cash, in this difficult time, to our colleges and universities? Of course they will!

Business people, even as they master the art of working with schools of higher education to serve their own best interests—as well as those of the nation—are also going to have to become a lot shrewder and a lot more demanding about what gets done with the money they contribute. Universities and colleges need to bid for contributions— and need to learn the fine art of making those bids highly competitive. They are also going to have to master the fine art of reporting on how those funds have been spent—in reports that can actually stand up, if necessary, to the most unexpected of audits and critiques.

The so-called "walls" separating business and education—those myths of the postwar period—have come crashing down like Jericho's. Let's hope now that business and education can combine their efforts in a serious partnership—one strong enough to deal even with this ever-so-serious decade.

I believe at risk is our national future, so dependent on our national system of higher education. And if those who work in higher education can finally bring themselves to *understand* that risk—and can actually *respond* to the gun barrel now pressed against their temples—*then* will come the moment for business to "give its all" where our colleges and universities are concerned. The ultimate beneficiary will be our country. The ultimate beneficiary will be each one of us as we hopefully recover the dynamism with which America used to be synonymous.

Then Gulliver will arise at last, and show the world what he can do.

ESSAY PUBLISHED IN THE WORLD & I MAGAZINE
DECEMBER 1991*

THE DIFFICULT QUEST FOR BALANCE IN AMERICAN HIGHER EDUCATION

"*Universities have lost their immunity* from public criticism," Robert Rosenzweig, president of the prestigious Association of American Universities (AAU) recently declared. "There's no longer a presumption in favor of their virtue."

What made his remark so significant was the fact that the AAU represents precisely the major research universities—the "biggies"—that for several decades have ruled the roost of American higher education, setting the standards not only for less renowned universities but, increasingly, for four-year colleges as well, including those long praised for their devotion to teaching and the liberal arts.

As all university and college presidents have long been aware, nationally and internationally recognized research—rather than successful teaching of undergraduates—has been and is the key to obtaining truly major funding from the federal government, the big foundations, and the kinds of individual donors whose gifts run into the seven and eight figures. Indeed, it has also long been the key to attracting applications for the research universities' undergraduate colleges, even after years of complaint about the fact that the Great Researchers themselves seldom appear in an undergraduate classroom, while teaching is conducted—to a great extent—by teaching assistants, often very harassed ones whose primary concerns are their own studies as well as their often precarious economic status. To which can be added, if they were educated abroad, their limited command of English and the resulting complaints from students and families drawn to their universities by the credentials of senior professors that can turn out to mean so little where the teaching of undergraduates is concerned!

THE VOLCANO ERUPTS (1988-1991)

The biggies having had their way for such a long time, and having acquired a certain reputation for indifference to complaint, nevertheless focused their collective attention when Rosenzweig confirmed that they have now been brought sharply down to earth—into the rank and file of those whom the U.S. Congress and the individual state legislatures now regard as legitimate targets of investigation, with the majority of Americans lending support, whether enthusiastic or reluctant, to their inquisitive representatives. Escalating tuition costs for their children's higher education have swept away the last vestiges of the awed acquiescence "average Americans" may once have felt they owed to all those caps, gowns, maces and higher degrees.

Terra firma, for institutions so unused to it, has proven to be unfamiliar ground. Schools founded in the seventeenth and eighteenth centuries, from Harvard and Yale to Princeton and Columbia, or as bastions of civic significance amid the westward expansion of the nineteenth century, are suddenly being accorded no more *automatic* respect than is paid to such other formerly "sacred" professions as medicine and banking.

In the unexpected manner that so often characterizes true as opposed to merely imagined historical events, the kinetic spark that finally set this country's higher education scene ablaze had nothing to do with earlier issues—the neglect of undergraduate teaching, the unintelligible lectures allegedly delivered by some teaching assistants, or even the fact that a strong devotion to teaching rather than research is said to be a certain route to career suicide for professors and to budgetary malaise for their schools. Instead, the issue that galvanized America's attention turned out to be that of "research overhead," the billings to federal agencies for "indirect costs," by, in the first instance, Stanford University, and then, the American public was soon informed, by many *other* biggies as well.

What the "overhead issue" seemed to etch into the public mind was not only that major universities and their funding sources had committed specific blunders but, given the bizarre nature of some of the expenditures billed to Washington, that America's major research universities *could no longer be trusted.* Suddenly the doors have been flung open to a host of other suspicions as well, until even schools with entirely "clean hands" can be forgiven the feeling that they are corralled in a dock where, contrary to the most fundamental principles of Anglo-Saxon jurisprudence, they must continually prove themselves innocent in order not to be presumed guilty.

The extent of the crisis can be judged from the names of some of the universities being "talked to" by the federal government. These names include Harvard, Yale, Johns Hopkins, Carnegie-Mellon, the University of Pittsburgh, Columbia, Cornell, M.I.T., the California Institute of Technology, Dartmouth, Duke, Emory, the University of Pennsylvania, the University of Texas, the University of Southern California, the University of Hawaii, Rutgers and Washington University in St. Louis—some of whom are moving swiftly to visit Washington before Washington visits them.

Meanwhile, the items previously billed as "indirect costs" of research, and now the subjects of public *mea culpas*, include, to the outrage or amusement of the American public, Neiman-Marcus crystal decanters, executive jet service for a university president whose height made him "uncomfortable" in the seats assigned to ordinary people on regular commercial flights, and travel expenses incurred by a university president's spouse in visits to Caribbean resorts and to football matches in Ireland.

What was abruptly brought to a close by the "research overhead" scandal was the period, extending from the end of the Second World War to the beginning of the final decade of the twentieth century, when Americans conducted an unprecedented love affair with their universities—schools that had grown far more accustomed, in the nineteenth and twentieth centuries, to the feral and paranoid anti-intellectualism identified by the late Richard Hofstadter as one of the major themes of American political life.

THE BEGINNING OF THE END (1980-1988)

The beginning of the end, where America's postwar love affair with higher education was concerned, can be seen in retrospect as the time only a decade or so ago when President Reagan appointed William Bennett to be U.S. secretary of education and gave him his head regarding the nation's universities and colleges. Bennett was soon commuting from coast to coast, with many stops in between, to bring his message home to the American people. Higher education had become a sink of corruption, he declared, where bloated bureaucracies practiced the fine art of doing nothing, at length, for steadily rising rates of pay. He was conspicuously successful in this role.

The pace set by Bennett was further speeded up by the publication, in 1988, of Charles J. Sykes's book, *ProfScam: Professors and the Demise of Higher Education*. Initially derided and ignored by the higher education community, Sykes's book, as it became a juicy plum of the lecture and TV talk show circuit, soon developed into a dragon that higher education spokesmen had to slay again and again and again. Sykes's drift was soon seconded and supported by such books as Roger Kimball's *Tenured Radicals: How Politics Has Corrupted Our Higher Education*, Page Smith's *Killing the Spirit: Higher Education in America*, and Sykes's second book, *The Hollow Men: Politics and Corruption in Higher Education*, all of which were published in 1990. And, even as the "research overhead" issue blazed its way across the front pages and the TV news, the literary *coup de grace* was delivered by Dinesh D'Souza's book *Illiberal Education: The Politics of Race and Sex on Campus*, which was published early in 1991—even as the Anxious Nineties were convincing middle-class Americans that their once *relatively* secure world had now turned as slippery and insecure as that long experienced by blue-collar employees working for an hourly wage, and that they too could find themselves slipping from middle-class status into the American "underclass." Only look, D'Souza's text implied, at what a higher education "scene" you and your kids are getting in return for the escalating tuitions you can barely afford!

As a result, D'Souza found himself being swept up in a tidal wave of public response and general approval. Countless syndicated columnists, television commentators and editorial writers in the country joined in making his name nearly as familiar to Americans as that of Madonna or Larry Bird. The earlier front-page and editorial-page harangues on the subject of "research overhead" now gave way to the subjects of D'Souza's chapters, which include "The Victim's Revolution on Campus," "In Search of Black Pharaohs,"

"The New Censorship" (or "P.C."), and "Tyranny of the Minority."

And the concluding crescendo of D'Souza's "final symphonic movement" was delivered by no less than the president of the United States, in a commencement address at the University of Michigan that the *Washington Times* summed up with the headline (May 6, 1991): " 'Political Correctness' Gets a Presidential Chastising."

The president of the United States received cheers and applause, the *Times* reported, "when he used a weekend commencement speech. . .to attack the bruising of the First Amendment under the guise of 'political correctness' on the nation's college campuses." As usual, Bush's timing was excellent. His speech was reported, within a few days, to have markedly accelerated Congress's interest in this subject—and it served, in effect, as the overture to his and his administration's concern with the matter of "quotas." (Universities—most notably Georgetown, via its law school, but every other school of higher education as well, since all are struggling for greater student "diversity"—are, of course, near the center of the "quota" debate as well.)

Where American higher education is concerned, Americans have had, it appears, "more than enough." What might have gone unnoticed in more prosperous times sticks out like the proverbial sore thumb in a time of economic anxiety like the present. And where America's higher *educators* are concerned, the Contrition Phase is now upon us, in which the characteristic question is "Whose fault was it?" and the quest for scapegoats leads to the public shaming of those who made themselves vulnerable when they became the stellar "success stories" of only a few years before.

Without getting into insoluble issues of "fault," we *can* allow ourselves to ask how all of this came to pass. How did American schools of higher education, admired throughout the world for their effectiveness and their resources, become subject to such scathing and sometimes exaggerated criticism on native ground? For an answer to that question, we must go all the way back to the 1950s, when anti-intellectualism faded into the social background and the postwar academic expansion moved into full speed.

THE LAVA BUILDS UP (1960-1980)

In the 1950s, universities and colleges were still rather insular places—often satirized, indeed, as "ivory towers" far removed from, and in some ways insulated against, the realities of the business world and of the "average American's" concerns.

In the 1960s, a major change took place. Even from those in no way categorizable as student or faculty "radicals," our schools of higher education began to receive praise for the degree to which they were profoundly *involved* with American society and actively *engaged* in meeting its needs. Clark Kerr coined the phrase "multiversity" to describe the new phenomenon—the university spilling out in all directions in order to serve the needs of the expanding American economy. The knee-jerk denunciations that followed from so many academic sources—wasn't multiversity the most vulgar sort of neologism, nothing but jargon and cant?—were an accurate indicator that Kerr had hit a sensitive nerve; probably by accurately describing a *de facto* reality that would soon be *de jure* as well?

Because in the late 1950s and the early 1960s, at so many individual universities and colleges, and regardless of the specific department and/or subject under discussion, it was clear to nearly everyone that the academic center of gravity was shifting from undergraduate education to postgraduate research, from the B.A. degree to the Ph.D., and from academic breadth in the traditional liberal arts mode to ever-intensifying levels of disciplinary and subdisciplinary specialization.

And as those changes occurred, it seemed perfectly natural that universities should, in the manner envisioned by Kerr, serve the commercial and governmental needs of the society that supported them, ideologically and politically as well as economically. Indeed, the raging (sometimes rampaging!) "student radicals" who only a few years later were denouncing universities and colleges for "selling out to the military-industrial complex" *also* said they wanted higher education to involve itself more deeply with American society—only in order to serve the needs of America's poor and deprived citizens rather than the needs of its Fortune 500 corporations.

Nor did the great academic shift of the 1970s from curricular to budgetary concerns—which grew out of the Arab oil embargo and the subsequent period of high inflation—significantly alter this underlying assumption. True, university-based business schools, virtual pariahs in the academic status system of the 1950s, now ruled the academic roost. True, the M.B.A. now rivaled the Ph.D. as the "degree of choice." But what that really amounted to was a *redefinition* of America's greatest need—as being the need for competent business managers and executives rather than competent teachers of English literature or competent social workers and fiery crusaders on behalf of the poor—rather than any reversal of the notion that universities and colleges were now, and *should* be, somewhere near the "core" of America's struggle to cope with the challenges of the modern world.

But the move to the "core" or "center" brought with it two inevitable side effects that reversed everything implied by the earlier usage "Ivory Tower." First, what goes on at the center as opposed to the periphery is automatically subject to public interest and inspection, especially when it involves the expenditure of taxpayer money. Which is why the "core" metaphor can so easily be replaced by that of a goldfish bowl. And secondly, one cannot invite oneself "out into the world" without also inviting the world—and its many serious problems—"inside."

As teachers and researchers began, in and after the 1950s, to receive salaries and fringe benefits within hailing distance of corporate norms (at least where middle management was concerned), and as tuition began to increase accordingly, "attention," to paraphrase *Death of a Salesman*, did indeed "begin to be paid." The attention was limited, at first, to an intellectual elite, mainly based on the east and west coasts, for whom higher education was a potential source of employment as well as an altruistic social concern. But as college degrees became mandatory even for those seeking entry-level jobs, and as the percentage of American high school graduates attending universities and colleges steadily grew, more and more Americans were, of course, drawn into the "circle of concern"—until Secretary Bennett, when he climbed into the saddle, found something like a "mass audience" awaiting his denunciations.

Meanwhile, the rise of a whole new set of nationwide political concerns was accurately reflected or refracted—like all major social and political phenomena—in the American academic microcosm attended by the majority of the nation's late adolescents. With our campuses as "center stage," a position easily communicated by the media's "eyes" and "ears," the "higher education drama" seemed to reach nearly Shakespearean proportions. By the time the fiscal scandals of the 1980s and early 1990s began to penetrate the cracking facades of an earlier academic image—that of the gentle "Halls of Ivy," populated by absentminded professors engaged in communing with "higher concerns"—a whole society had its attention riveted to the screen on which college professors and university presidents were suddenly "starred."

What our schools of higher education now reflected was an America increasingly polarized between narrow ethic and class concerns, a society that more and more resembled the fissuring landscape created by a major earthquake. Every *potential* split—between men and women, blacks and whites, Asians and Hispanics, gays and "straights," the "center-city poor" and the "suburban affluent," "Western Tradition conservatives" and "Third World radicals"—seemed suddenly to enter a kinetic phase, till syndicated columnists and television commentators began to sound like the chorus in a Greek tragedy, bemoaning the onset of chaos in place of a former order.

And needless to say, these broad social developments seemed especially alarming in the *academic* context because, all specific disillusionments aside, that was *still* ostensibly the American environment that alone was fully dedicated to reason and dispassionate analysis. And so it came to be that America's universities and colleges were easily scapegoated as one of the chief *causes*, rather than as among the most serious *victims*, of America's vast new panorama of Big Trouble.

AND THE CURRENT ACADEMIC RESPONSE . . .

It is a truism to observe that academicians are more inclined toward the liberal than the conservative end of the political spectrum. And one endemic side effect of liberalism, both its sympathizers and its critics agree, is the tendency to be afflicted with irrational levels of guilt—to take on, in effect, "global" levels of responsibility and concern that cannot be dealt with on an individual basis.

The results of that tendency have long been visible in the academic world. Policy-making, down to quite simple levels of decision, has often proceeded at a snail's pace because of this tendency to see cosmic issues of justice and responsibility in even the simplest decisions. (In higher education, indeed, shifts of authority from faculty to administrative governance can usually be accounted for by the need to get decisions actually *made*—especially in a time as economically and politically stressful as the present.)

As the anti-higher education mood in the nation has intensified, therefore, the results, where academic morale is concerned, have been predictably dire. It's not easy, with an already guilt-laden mind-set, to deal with the fact that one's morning newspaper is once again featuring some heavy criticism of one's profession, quite possibly on the front page or in a nationally syndicated column. It's even harder, if one works for a *public* university or college, to deal with the fact that the exceedingly painful higher education cutbacks announced by the governor *last* month will probably have to be doubled—possibly tripled—because the state budgetary crisis is so much worse than was previously calculated.

And whether one's salary comes from a public or an independent institution of higher education, it's been hardest of all, in the past few years, to deal with the fact that so much bad news has been arriving all at once. *Besides* the suspicions generated by the "research overhead" controversy, *besides* the fiscal crisis that has affected even Harvard, Yale, Stanford and other schools whose capital endowments are in the billions, and *besides* all the ethnic and political fractures that have been keeping so many campuses on edge ("A blowup just around the corner?"), we can list:

A. Growing challenges to the very existence, on our campuses, of various enterprises, including bookstores and food stores, that compete with local businesses selling the same or similar items. Those enterprises, local merchants have become increasingly insistent in emphasizing, enjoy tax-exempt status that represents unfair competition for them. The logical conclusion of their arguments: that such tax exemptions be selectively withdrawn when "profit-making" is the issue. At stake, of course, are not just profits, when and if those are in fact being realized on a regular basis, but student morale. The decision to shut down even a grossly unprofitable campus enterprise can have serious side effects, especially on schools located in "outer suburban" or rural areas, where alternative shopping requires a great deal of commuting.

B. A variety of problems generated by intercollegiate sports, especially the significant money levels now involved in televised athletics and the exploitation of minority athletes who too often fail to obtain their degrees. These problems have led to (a) the current round of deliberations by the National Collegiate Athletic Association (NCAA), and (b) some lurid media coverage that has arrived at "precisely the wrong time."

C. The fact that the American public has now been regaled, over a period of several years, with a media theme that has become a virtual daily leitmotif: the extent to which American graduates fail to match up to the skill- and knowledge-levels of their European and Asian counterparts. Though *most* of the criticism is being directed at the nation's public elementary and high schools, generous quantities have washed over into the world of higher education as well.

D. The fact that specific campus controversies over curricular, intellectual and social issues—which include political correctness (PC), teaching vs. research, deconstructionist literary and artistic theory, multiculturalism, diversity, free speech vs. civility, the Western Tradition as opposed to a wide variety of "other traditions," campus security, professorial work hours and work habits, unethical and sometimes illegal behavior by specific university presidents, and questionable fund-raising practices—have helped to further intensify the general sense that "something's rotten in the state of American higher education" and that drastic governmental surgery of some kind may soon be required.

E. Growing unhappiness on the part of black commentators in particular, figures ranging from William Raspberry to Thomas Sowell and Shelby Steele, over the fact that *any* career success enjoyed by a black executive or technician or other award-winner is now automatically attributed to affirmative action or "quotas," a trend that has developed both inside and outside the academic world. A deadly spiral is thus set going. As a result, black strivers never feel that they have achieved "enough" to convince whites—whites as a *group*—that they are in fact as authentic, and as entitled to respect, as their white and Asian counterparts.

One consequence of this tragic back-and-forth? Increasingly, Steele argues in his book *The Content of Our Character* (1990), blacks cling to "an adversarial victim-focused identity that preoccupies us with white racism." Blacks are willy-nilly drawn into a view of life in which it is their inescapable destiny to be passively and unjustly manipulated rather than admitted to the charmed circle of American society's movers and shakers. And the result within institutions of higher education in particular, senior administrators at many universities and colleges will confirm, is often for black student and faculty activists to defeat their own causes by refusing even the most obvious alliances and concessions. "No compromise" thus leads, as is so often the case in life, to no victory, either—or to a victory of the Pyrrhic sort, when onlookers can cynically whisper that "they" got their way in the "usual" fashion, rather than reasoned argument and adroit negotiation. Whereupon the spiral gets yet another boost in its tragic downward hurtle.

Surveying the full panoply of depressing issues that now confront higher education in the United States, I am personally amazed that the majority of teachers and administrators continue to function in a reasonable, often commendable, fashion. A few years ago they were caricatured as lost in the impractical, abstract spaces of the "Ivory Tower." That was a libel even then, given the intense kinds of critical scrutiny to which academicians have always subjected one another. Now they are being criticized for allowing politics to elbow intellect aside. But the most relevant image for today's collective "faculty position" might be that of a submarine doggedly continuing on course despite the mines, bombs and torpedoes going off all around its dented hull!

But academic morale, all voices testify and all perspectives agree, tends to be lower today than at any time since the Great Depression. The "victim psychology" so often denounced in the media appears to be claiming yet one more victim—which is bad news for those of us trying hard to turn defeatism and depression around.

LIFE IN A WORLD OF MEDIA MAVENS

"Scholars who study the press," declared a front-page article in *The Chronicle of Higher Education* on June 12, 1991, "see the furor over political correctness—which has reached the covers of the *Atlantic*, *Newsweek*, and *New Yorker* magazines—as a case of media overkill. But they point out that it reflects larger anxieties, and could even be used as an issue in political campaigns.

" 'Once a media panic of this sort emerges, there's no way to fight it,' said Todd Gitlin, professor of sociology at the University of California at Berkeley, who called the coverage 'pack journalism of the worst sort.'

"Mr. Gitlin. . .said some of the abuses on campuses were real and deserved scrutiny. But the sweeping label of political correctness, which implies a uniform set of left-wing values, presumes that one can't have differing views on particular matters. 'It combines race anxiety with anti-intellectualism and university bashing,' Mr. Gitlin said."

Was this article, here and in other passages, missing something quite major? Indeed it was, and the "something," to which I will add a number of smaller but still significant *things*, was well summed up by a friend who has worked extensively in both corporate and academic communications:

"Time was," he recently observed, "when one could make quite a decent living just teaching people the 'basics' of publicity work: how to draft a press release, what it needed to look like in order to be taken seriously by an editor at a copy desk, how its first two sentences would receive about three seconds of scrutiny—a critical three seconds—before it was directed into either the circular file or the pile of 'possibles,' and how to interest a local or regional television or radio station in giving one's prize event, be it a press conference or an auction of rare antique thimbles, 'some coverage.'

"Today," he went on, "in our media-saturated world, that draws us *inside* its categories and fantasies like some deadly charm in a grown-up fairy tale, that same body of knowledge is 'taken in with one's mother's milk,' so to speak. University administrators reel as the television crews and the print reporters storm onto campus to cover yet *another* 'radical' demonstration, complete with picket-signs and clenched fists, by some politico/ethnico/social-reform 'splinter group' with a total of 12 members, only four of whom pay their dues—but whose 'feel' for how to set up a 30-second TV and radio 'bite' is as good as that of the White House staff. Indeed, the main problem for the still and video photographers is to get enough fists into their camera angles so that viewers who catch the 'bite' don't realize how few demonstrators there really were!"

Thus, the majority of American university and college presidents have probably, by now, shared the experience of sitting across a desk from one or another "activist" leader and having the latter threaten to "bring the press in," usually at some critical point in the academic calendar when (a) high school seniors and their families are in the process of deciding whether or not to enroll, and/or (b) a major private foundation is deciding whether or not to renew its annual grant to the university, and/or (c) a gaggle of "influentials" that includes the governor of the state is expected on campus for a major conference.

"Strong-arm" tactics? That, alas, was the terminology of an earlier and simpler age. Today, in "our media-saturated world"—which has discommoded the very sense of a firm, unchanging, bedrock "reality" not subject to continuous emendation and frequent reversal—what may once have been characterized as the tactics of an Al Capone have become something like a daily norm—one experienced *most* sharply in the academic world, which Americans still expect, at some level, to be a nobler and more idealistic milieu than the fallen universe "outside the walls" where most of them live and work.

Nor does the "media challenge" come at universities and colleges solely from a "student radical" direction. Faculty members of every imaginable persuasion have also learned to "leak" information or opinions to the local media that, in turn, are particularly eager to snap these morsels up—and are sometimes willing to cite them, in direct quotes or through paraphrase, without attribution to anyone in particular. Or the source might be listed as an "untenured professor who asked that his/her name not be used, lest he/she suffer retribution."

Or the source might be "a disgruntled staff member" rather than a professor, administrator or student.

At any rate, what *The Chronicle* conspicuously failed to communicate was the very large truth that the media got used to being invited onto campus, or to give its internal politics coverage via telephone calls, long before the media engaged in what Professor Gitlin characterizes as their wicked "overkill." Academicians who failed to slam on the brakes when *only* senior administrators were being maligned on the six-o'clock news or the front page of the local newspaper should not wax quite so selfrighteous now that public interest has also discovered *them*.

The fact is that the media are seldom arbitrary when they spend huge sums to transport all that expensive equipment, together with its human handlers, to particular sites "in or around town." When they direct their crews to the local college or university, they do so because their highly paid brains have weighed all the available "news opportunities" and have decided that that campus is looking, once again, very "juicy"!

Which leads me to the second point so blithely passed over by Professor Gitlin. The late Richard Hofstadter, as I noted above, was the author of a book on anti-intellectualism as a main current—and a consistent one—in American political life. If the media are spearheading a revival of this historical tendency—something they would do only after a very sophisticated analysis of current attitudes among the members of their audience, then all of those on academic payrolls have reason to be apprehensive about their individual futures and collective future.

One more quotation from this article in *The Chronicle of Higher Education* and I am done with it. Having delivered himself of the remarks I have quoted above, Professor Gitlin added: "People who don't know the difference between Plato and NATO get to sneer at academics and pretend they're defenders of the cultural tradition."

Could Evelyn Waugh or D.H. Lawrence have done any better a job of pillorying, by personifying, what has on so many occasions been called, fairly or unfairly, "typical academic arrogance"? True, there are folks around who can't tell Plato from NATO and Pluto the Pup from

Pluto the reigning divinity of the Roman underworld. But even such degraded ignoramuses know where to cast their ballots at election time and those for whom they will vote—as opposed to those whom they will ignore—are politicians profoundly in touch with what their constituents are currently feeling. And the latter, in turn, vote on higher education bills of the sort that affect even Professor Gitlin.

A FEW SPECIFICS—AND A BRIEF CONCLUSION

I have tried to communicate a broad yet detailed sense of the challenges facing American higher education in the final decade of the twentieth century. What our universities and colleges are struggling to achieve is a difficult balance between competing priorities, each of which comes imbued with its own sense of urgency. They are being asked, among other things, to provide better and wider access for minority applicants; to take account of cultural heritages that differ radically from that of the West; to keep their books balanced at a time when that is a challenge even for Fortune 500 corporations; to hold down tuition increases; to improve undergraduate teaching; to keep up the research that has been so important, especially over the last half century, for the American economy; and to see to it that intracampus ethnic and political divisions, reflecting the tensions of the entire society, do not interfere with academic functioning. Balance will not be achieved without considerable effort and resourcefulness.

Meanwhile, here are some of the specific issues with which our schools of higher education will have to deal as they approach the third millennium:

A. Curriculum. Universities and colleges are going to have to find a viable middle ground between the positions represented by the National Association of Scholars on the one hand and by a wide variety of curricular reformers on the other. The majority on both sides of the dispute—those who want to preserve a "core curriculum" based on our Western cultural heritage, and those who desire radical change in this "traditional" approach—have scored some valid points. Individuals in the opposing camps have also said some very silly things that will look even sillier in retrospect. But the likelihood of achieving compromise and balance seems to me very good, and the grounds for compromise have already been laid. That they are not more visible is due in large part to the fact that conflict rather than conciliation is regarded as "media-worthy" by the media themselves.

B. Teaching and research. Here, the foundations for compromise already bear some actual "building weight." As universities and colleges learn to share their resources, research costs will come down. Teaching, meanwhile, has achieved a cachet that would have seemed most unlikely even two or three years ago. Indeed, major research universities like Stanford are now in the forefront of the schools promising, at long last, to reward excellent teaching the way they have rewarded, until recently, relatively mediocre research. And the "new day a-dawning" will come as good news not only to undergraduates and their families but to the 80 percent or so of American faculty members who regularly confide, to nationwide polls, that their research and publishing has a lot more to do with the desire for advancement than the quest for truth.

Indeed, what we now need to keep in mind is that good teaching is always based on the type of instructorial energy and commitment that make a personal "research program" almost mandatory. And while good research *can* be conducted by those indifferent or hostile toward the "waste of time" involved in teaching, it is a great deal more common for the enthusiasm and commitment of a well-motivated researcher to "overflow." The beneficiaries of this process may be research assistants or undergraduates—but beneficiaries there will be.

C. Budget and marketing. Broad generalizations of any kind are especially difficult in this area since—even in the difficult years of the 1990s, at a time when even Harvard's $5 *billion-plus* capital endowment has proven insufficient to prevent that university's annual budget from sliding, for the first time in living memory, into the red— there are schools experiencing no financial problems whatsoever. Indeed, some of these capital-endowed fortunates are actively luring academic "superstars" from other universities with salaries and fringe benefits reminiscent of Wall Street in the 1980s.

But universities share one serious flaw. They, and their faculty members in particular, distrust anything that smacks too conspicuously of advertising or marketing.

At a critical time like the present, when most academic budgets are under such serious pressure that talk of terminating untenured and sometimes tenured faculty has become common, our universities and colleges also share a flaw with American industry—the tendency to spend a lot more on marketing when enrollments (=sales) are booming than when they are in retreat. That, of course, has long been acknowledged by industry analysts to represent a 180-degree error.

Budgetary balance in the academic context must be a balance conducive to the long-term survival and viability of the specific school being—yes—*marketed* to its potential students and their families. Resource allocations here must not be cut back without the most serious self-examination. And at the same time, those resources must be allocated in such a way as to enlist design talents so keen as to know how to avoid any appearance of ostentation or waste in the marketing materials they produce and their academic employer uses. If that seems "dishonest" by the standards used in teaching and research, then they in turn can be called "ineffective" by the standards of what a school's enrollment needs so often require.

D. Student relations (including minority student relations). Here, of course, is a minefield so strewn with danger as to resemble the dreadful "no-man's-land" of the First World War. Students with any kind of a grievance, students "of color" or "without color," have learned how to use the media in order to embarrass their schools— greatly aided by the fact that society is so involved with, uncertain about, and sometimes fearful of its adolescent members that they and their behaviors are "always news." Though the future of student relations will depend on the wisdom, goodwill, sense of justice and empathic capabilities of faculty members and administrators, it will depend to an equal and sometimes even greater extent on the degree to which students can manifest these same qualities.

That was definitely *not* true from the eighteenth century through the first half of the twentieth—when the medieval and somewhat later pattern of "town-gown riots" moved into abeyance. It has definitely been true since the 1960s. And the quest for balance in the area of student relations, including minority relations, is therefore a Goliath-sized IF.

Balance: from the ancient Greeks to the present final decade of the second millennium, an ideal more often praised than realized. "Nothing to excess!" insisted the habitually excessive Hellenes and their many predecessors and successors. Whether souls as enlightened as we have now become will do better—*that* remains to be seen.

What is most urgent at the present time is the rebuilding of internal academic morale, because little can be achieved when the people who must do the achieving feel mired in depression and helplessness. To carry out some highly necessary academic reforms in a *non*punitive, *non*counterproductive manner is the most immediate task facing the academic world and its critics.

1992

AMERICAN HIGHER EDUCATION CONFRONTS ITS FRAYED SELF-IMAGE

To discuss "American Higher Education Confronts Its Frayed Self-Image," I have drawn upon a tale straight out of the *Thousand-and-One Nights.*

It's the fable of an academic system—a system consisting of America's specialized postgraduate institutes, universities, four-year colleges, community colleges and technical colleges—a system that supports both public and private versions of these schools—a system that is the envy, at each and every one of these levels, of the schools and governments in every other part of our planet—and a system that deserves to be numbered among the genuine wonders of the modern world.

It's a fable about how a profoundly pervasive higher education system such as the world has never seen before—one perfectly attuned, moreover, to the demographic and pedagogical realities of the nation that has developed it—ended up feeling neither fabulous nor virtuous nor functional, but just as if it were a large, slimy, wart-covered and profoundly ugly *frog,* one who sat on his lily-pad from morning to night and croaked, in that throaty voice of his: "O where is the Fairy Godmother whose kiss will turn me back into a handsome prince?"

Well, one day who should come flying by—as you might expect in a distinguished lecture of *this* particular sort—but a wise old owl. And being an owl from Washington, what he had in his beak was neither a clump of tasty berries nor an olive branch but, of course, a couple of newspaper *clippings.*

The frog didn't miss a beat. He ceased his croaking and cried, "Dear Mr. Owl, what do those clippings say that might help to rescue me from the sad state I'm in." The owl promptly landed on a branch and replied, "Well, the first one appeared in *The Washington Post* only a few days ago, and its headline reads, 'A HIDDEN U.S. EXPORT: HIGHER EDUCATION.' And it's all about the extent to which Asian students are flocking to the United States rather than to Japan for their higher educations. 'While Asian companies making various high-tech gadgets and low-tech widgets have been clobbering American firms,' the article says at one point, 'and Asian schoolchildren have been surpassing their American counterparts in math tests, young Asian adults are concluding in record numbers that the United States is the number one competitor at providing university-level study.'

"And the second clipping is a Post editorial that appeared a few days later, on February 21st. Its title is 'Scholar Diplomacy,' and the first paragraph reads,

'Cramped by the recession and by federal cutbacks, universities are increasingly weighing the option of streamlining and occasionally eliminating their advanced programs. Congress meanwhile is pursuing allegations that leading graduate departments overspent and overbilled the government on scientific research. In this landscape of self-doubt and decline, it's easy to lose sight of the fact that, on the international scene, American graduate education continues to enjoy unchallenged mastery. This is true especially in such fields as the hard sciences, math, computers and high technology—just those fields that, outside academia, are usually spoken of as U.S. weaknesses.'

"And," the owl concluded, "the editorial adds to the Asian students those 'from India, Pakistan and, increasingly, the Middle East, parts of the world that traditionally looked to Oxford and Cambridge.'"

Now the frog was *really* depressed. Being a higher-education-type frog, he proceeded, with the owl as audience, to develop a long and windy analogy between America's present role in relation to the world's most expansion-minded economies and that of ancient Greece to ancient Rome. And he'd gotten as far as a comparison between modern American presidents and the successors of Alexander the Great when I came along, armed to the gills with my stainless steel *chutzpah*, and proceeded to enlighten both Froggy and his well-feathered interlocutor. I will now recite the text of my remarks as they flowed from me that day:

Look, I began, the first point all this stuff is implicitly making is the extent to which American higher education in the 1990s is *still* in bondage to the public elementary and secondary schools. That was true in 1955, when I was a freshman in college, and the professors regarded it as their prime duty to break open the mildewed carapace of mediocrity inside of which each and every one of us had been embalmed during the high school years. And it's true in 1992, when the sheer amount of *talk* about public elementary and secondary education could replace Niagara as a source of hydroelectric power while the amount of measurable annual *accomplishment*—leaving aside Boston University and the Chelsea School District, of course—couldn't blow a dandelion seed from one end of the bathtub to another.

Here we are in a major, though possibly declining, industrial power where everybody agrees that we've got to do something about our public education system—everybody from the President of the United States to the CEO's of Fortune 500 companies to the supermarkets and fast-food emporia looking for part-time employees—yet nothing, or next to nothing, actually *happens*. It's no problem to mobilize force on an apocalyptic scale in order to put down Saddam Hussein. It's an *insoluble* problem, meanwhile, to produce graduating classes of high school seniors who can actually take advantage of what our universities have to offer. What they have to offer gets kidnapped by students from every *other* part of the world and carried back to *their* homelands. Meanwhile, Americans get agitated about the money being repatriated to *Japan*, of all places, whose American-based plants and American employees offer one of the few points of sunshine in today's American national economy.

And behind the failure of the American public schools—behind the *tolerance* of their ongoing failure—there surely lies a pattern of profound failure by the *parents* of America's schoolchildren, the very people who then uncritically lap up the media presentation of our universities and colleges as centers of sin that make Sodom and Gomorrah look like *convents* by comparison!

And having done with my preliminaries, what I'm going to argue is that the American inability to deal with the education of our children at the elementary and secondary levels has a kind of malign complement in the American tendency to treat higher education in magical or fetishistic terms—as a place *onto which to project all kinds of contradictory wishes, hopes and demands*. I will try to do justice to the extent to which these projections help to account for a *lot* of the demoralization we see around us in our universities and four-year colleges. But rather than absolve our schools of higher education in toto, I will also acknowledge specific failures that can be traced to our faculty members and administrators.

I'll start with what seems to me an unassailable fact: the extent to which our universities are now suffering from a sense of *conflicted mission*.

Unlike most professionals in our society, unlike physicians, lawyers and engineers, for example, those who now work under the title of *professor* are very often deeply uncertain as to what *exactly* they ought to be doing. Their uncertainty doesn't spring, obviously, from any lack of brain-power or analytic capacity. It springs, rather, from the contradictory missions and mandates that those of us who work in higher education are receiving, *right now*, from the American public.

Should our schools of higher education be emphasizing research missions and goals of demonstrated importance—missions that may prove critical to the innovative power of the American economy, and therefore to America's position in the *international* economy?

Or do they need to focus on what amounts to mass remedial education, as they seek to compensate for the failures of our nation's public schools?

Should they be focusing their attention—through the lens of their business schools—on the American economy's *internal* weaknesses, which have less to do with the frontiers of research than with the limitations of American *managers*, so many of whom hold M.B.A. degrees? If we concentrate our energies on the complex and expensive task of revolutionizing American business education, then *perhaps* we will be spared the humiliating spectacle of Japanese managers doing just as well with American workers as they do with those "back home," and turning out products of identical quality. But on the other hand, to what extent will a revolution here make it even clearer that the fault lies with the elementary and secondary systems in which our business students *also* make their educational start?

Or is it more important that our schools of higher education *directly* involve themselves with the public schools? And if so, how much more likely are they to succeed in the face of tenured teachers and principals locked into bureaucratic procedures that even Franz Kafka would have had trouble imagining? And can they in fact be effective if the problem lies as much in the thought-processes of American parents as in the scholastic weaknesses and prejudices of their children?

And finally, should this whole range of challenges and uncertainties lead us to conclude that present debates about the college curriculum—debates centered, typically, on such versus as *The Western Tradition vs. Multiculturalism*—add up to a complete red herring? If what our students and graduates most lack, as our nation struggles to compete in the bitterly competitive international economy, are quantitative, technical and mathematical skills, then should the overhaul of our curricula from top to bottom—from the postgraduate down to the kindergarten and pre-school level—be one that simply ignores the currently fashionable debates centered around literature, the humanities and the liberal arts?

Questions like these are particularly sharp-edged at a time when financial pressures emphasize the need for choice and the need, in our universities and colleges, for self-limitation and choice. Unlike the schools of yesteryear, we can no longer even pretend that each and every university can also be a *universe*, and that the smallest liberal arts college can graduate employable *universalists*—universalists, moreover, who have room in their heads for the hypothesis that Plato, Augustine, Dante, Shakespeare, Spinoza and Goethe are just a bunch of dead white males.

When we look out over a higher education landscape buffeted by winds like these—arguments that have to do with the very core of their functions, missions and goals—is it any wonder that so many of those bearing the title of *professor* seem to have 200-pound sacks on their shoulders? And when we sense that one of the most common demands now being made where our schools of higher education are concerned is that they *save the nation and the national economy*, regardless of what's going on every place *else* in the United States, is it in fact amazing that academicians so often give the impression of *not knowing what to do next*?

Once we have focused our own attention on the extent to which our universities and four-year colleges have the dubious honor of being regarded as saviors—saviors who can even carry out entirely contradictory missions—one particular dilemma now being discussed here, there and everywhere is transformed into just one more symptom of this sad state of affairs: the one referred to, over and over and over again, as *Teaching vs. Research*.

This particular debating-topic has no more substance than gossamer, in my opinion, and is simply a *non-subject*, because what we are in fact talking about is neither *real* teaching nor *real* research. Whatever else I've learned after several decades in higher education, I've learned that the best teachers are those deeply concerned with, and deeply interested in, their *subjects*. For people like that, subject-matter isn't an inert "canon," that one has to trundle into the classroom year after year. It's alive. It changes with the times. New questions get asked about it. New discoveries are made about the backgrounds that produced it. And lo and behold, it looks a lot different in 1992 than it did in 1982 or 1892!

And *research*? Whether it gets done in medicine and the "natural" sciences or in areas generally listed under headings like "the humanities," *all* of research is a form of science in the sense that *all* of it takes place on the *frontiers* of knowledge, at the point where the territory ahead is shrouded in mist, crammed with question-marks, and laced with doubt. Teaching and research, therefore, aren't antitheses at all, except in academic novels where silly subjects are propounded in ridiculous dissertations by doctoral candidates whose cynicism would dismay even Machiavelli!

But one thing is certain. Since the time of the Second World War, research narrowly defined—research seen strictly in terms of the so-called "hard" sciences and their technological derivatives—has been the key to bringing immense amounts of government money into university coffers. And that is why recent financial scandals having to do with billings for "research overhead" have left such a bad taste in American mouths. What has been shattered is nothing less than a quasi-religion that has flourished for almost the entire second half of the twentieth century. Several university presidents have now "gone under" as the ripples of this particular scandal have widened again and again. And it is possible that what will emerge at the end of this particular tunnel is a new system for doing scientific research in this country—a system of specialized institutes like Los Alamos rather than the one associated with our traditional universities.

The quasi-religion of well-financed scientific research, in turn, has had a lot to do with the hierarchy of American higher education as seen by high school seniors and their families, which has so much less to do with truth than with the domain of myth and image. A school like Harvard, for example, which like other "flagship" universities has received the largest sums in the way of government funding, projects the image of being "tops in research." It's associated, in the American mind, with faculty "heavies" who are either riding helicopters on their way to the White House or peering into microscopes that can spot the blush on an amoeba's cheek.

Attendance at a school like *that*, great numbers of American believe in their hearts and souls, is practically a guarantee of remunerative lifetime employment. Heads lost in such clouds of illusion, they sell their grandmothers into slavery, hock the family heirlooms, and send their kids to Harvard.

And guess what? At Harvard, their kids *don't* have the experience of sitting down to a quiet and inspirational cup of tea with John Kenneth Galbraith. They *don't* get loving personal attention from Nobel Prize winners in microbiology and astrophysics. And they *are* quite likely to find themselves sitting in a lecture-hall the size of a Roman arena, barely comprehending the remarks being delivered, in a tongue *resembling* English, by a teaching assistant from some other galaxy. And then the parents, the families and the students themselves have the *chutzpah to complain!*

They are in fact, as I've already suggested, self-victimized. Once we have seen American higher education as a screen onto which are projected a host of national fantasies, the fantasy of "a Harvard education" makes as much sense—as much *fantasy* sense, that is—as the former notion that attendance at West Point or Notre Dame would fill a boy up with "manliness."

Faculty members and administrators, as I noted, are suffering from *a failure of definition* as they try to cope with a range of American hopes, wishes and demands too vast to be fulfilled by mere mortal institutions. And the issue has been sharpened, of course—some would say poisoned—by the fact that higher education costs a lot more today than it used to. As all of us know, that's because faculty members, administrators and staff are no longer being paid at rates that presuppose a vow of poverty, and they are even receiving fringe benefits, like pension plans and medical coverage, that reduce the chances of their being left to die after they've finally passed out on the street.

But someone, obviously, has to pay, and those who pay, in the form of tuition or in other ways, feel more licensed than ever as they press home the full force of their contradictory hopes and expectations.

I've spoken so far about the challenges of *conflicted mission* that now bedevil our schools of higher education. I'd like to move on to a set of problems at least as serious, and perhaps even *more* serious: problems of management and governance.

Two or three decades have gone by since our universities were first described in terms formerly reserved for Fortune 500 companies, and the comparison has seemed more appropriate with each passing year. That's most obviously true where universities with capital endowments of a billion dollars or more are concerned. But it's increasingly true as well of those with mere *nine*-figure endowments, given the typical extent of their involvements in this country and abroad, and the degree to which those involvements affect the lives of people living in communities adjacent to university campuses.

In short, we have lived long enough to see the comparison with Fortune 500-level corporations itself become a cliché. Yet we have not lived long enough to see the end of archaic university modes of governance summed up by the phrase "shared governance." It's a phrase that continues to enjoy nearly sacred status in our schools of higher education, while the pace of faculty senate deliberations continues to dominate the rhythms of university-wide decision-making.

The fact is that we live in an increasingly tricky and dangerous world where, especially when significant amounts of money are involved, decision-making must often be very, very quick if disaster is to be circumvented.

The academic ideal that characterized an earlier period of American history—the ideal of ivied halls, through which portentous figures out of the world of business and finance made their slow way to the board room to "check out" the university's investment portfolio—has been practically reversed. Board members would have to be on campus 24 hours a day and seven days a week in order to keep up with the day-to-day transactions made in the business office, by a vice president who would have little difficulty in getting a good job on Wall Street, and under the supervision of a president who is sometimes criticized for being a more avid reader of financial reports than of contemporary fiction and poetry or ancient Hindu epics.

And so, in relentless fashion, our universities have divided into what the late C. P. Snow called "two cultures," one of which *works at decision-making* while the other *makes decisions*. And if the latter did otherwise, then the former would soon have reason to wonder whether or not a paycheck would ever again be in the works at "the usual time."

That is not, in my judgment, a healthy situation. Shared governance, in the absence of *shared responsibility*, will always have a certain hollow ring. And at the same time, there is no getting around the fact that when fiscal responsibility involves the intake of vast quantities of *information*—much of it in numerical form—no one involved in *true* shared governance will find that he or she has much time for research, or even an adequate amount of time to prepare for classroom teaching.

To which must be added, I fear, the issue of *risk-taking*. At a time when, with good reason, *all* investments are suspect to *some* extent, and *all* promises on matters of taxation, zoning, quality and cost need to be scrutinized with nearly paranoid skepticism—at a time like the *present*, in other words—those with an aversion to risk are more likely to be found at the middle management and staff levels than at the fiscal controls of a large organization, be it in the for-profit or not-for-profit category.

But the *"faculty culture"* in schools of higher education tends to be, for better or worse, a risk-*averse* culture. You don't get a Ph.D. or other major academic credential by a willingness to engage in breathtaking acrobatics. You don't publish articles in refereed journals by threatening the psychological stability of the referees, or even setting their heads mildly a-spin.

On the other hand, you *do* conduct the fiscal affairs of a contemporary school of higher education by emerging from your scrutiny of the more blood-curdling business pages in today's *Washington Post, Wall Street Journal* and *New York Times* with your anxieties sufficiently low and your morale sufficiently intact so that you can make rapid decisions, or rapid *decisions not to decide*, without risk of coronary damage, bleeding ulcers, or a serious addiction to alcohol.

All of which helps to explain why, when these "two university cultures" do meet, they so often start out by clashing. The slower-paced and infinitely deliberate "faculty culture" plays the role of the classical tortoise. Peering out from under its shell, it accuses Brother Rabbit of behaving in a merely flighty and erratic manner. Brother Rabbit, who gets paid for *avoiding* all the shrapnel and machine-gun fire that currently darkens the sky, may have to summon the chairman of the board and half of its members—the more financially credentialed ones—in his own defense. They, in turn, peering through the slits of their own Fortune 500 fortresses, will generally confirm that Brother Rabbit was in the right place at the right time and *out* of it by the time it turned deadly.

But "victories" won in such a context—in an internal dispute grounded in matters of style and lifetime socialization—are at least as counterproductive as defeats. Already sufficiently divided as they struggle to decide on their true function in today's America, universities are further divided when it comes to something as basic as the very *processes* of vital decision-making.

So far I have been talking about university governance, and the extent to which it can be *genuinely* shared in the world we inhabit today. Add questions of management, and even the title of this lecture may seem a trifle understated. For example, many faculty members still resent the notion that they are managed *at all* to any extent—

especially when it comes to matters like the definition of an appropriate workload.

And they continue to do this at a time when federal and state legislators, seconded by the *executive* agencies of federal and state government, are showing a steadily more intense interest in precisely this
matter of faculty workloads—a time, moreover, when even *The
Chronicle of Higher Education* can publish articles like the one that appeared in its issue dated February 19, 1992: "Tight Budgets Demand
Studies of Faculty Productivity," by Daniel T. Layzell, a research and
fiscal analyst for the Arizona Joint Legislative Budget Committee.
Layzell noted that:

" 'at a time when many states' economies are troubled—and demands on their public-health and welfare programs are increasing
dramatically as a result—the issue of faculty members' workloads
at public colleges and universities is being examined anew. At
least five states are actively looking into the issue.

"As states explore ways to do more with less, policy makers are
looking at all areas of state government for examples of non-pro-
ductivity or low productivity . . . Of course, when legislators start
looking at how faculty members spend their time, faculty members and administrators react defensively, raising concerns about
'institutional autonomy' and the need for state leaders to 'recognize differences in institutional missions.'

"Their underlying concern, however, is whether studies of faculty members' productivity will lead to budget cuts. Policy makers' interest in faculty workloads is believed to be the greatest when
states' fiscal constraints are the tightest."

Layzell was talking about the *public* schools of higher education that
enroll 80 percent of all American students. But can anyone doubt
that the so-called "privates" will inevitably be affected by the same
new climate of relentless scrutiny? They are rendered more vulnerable, after all, by every dollar they accept from a government source—
for research, for student aid, or for campus construction and maintenance—as well as by their formerly routine tax exemptions, now under increasing challenge from local governments desperate for revenue.

And yet, in the face of all this, faculty productivity is a subject, given current norms of university management, that is virtually tabu on our nation's campuses. Anticipatory steps of any kind are therefore impossible. Not until a new and government-mandated dispensation "kicks in the door," so to speak, will this issue acquire sufficiently obvious importance to be verbally acknowledged!

There are those, even today, who grow uncomfortable whenever academic matters are cast in a financial light. They would prefer that noble intellectual tasks, goals and missions come without price-tags. In that sense, the running comparison between universities and Fortune 500 corporations has had a very salutary impact. What we have come to understand is that universities, like major companies, are first and foremost limited financial systems in which everything has a price-tag, and in which "trade-offs" are a matter not of choice but necessity.

When a legislature tells a limited financial system to provide better access and facilities for the handicapped, *but doesn't vote any funding to make that possible*, then we can be certain there will be less money for books and/or academic facilities and/or salaries and/or fringe benefits—indeed, that jobs may be lost as a result. When municipalities attempt to tax hitherto-untaxed university real estate, they should not react with shock when the emergency facilities at the university's hospital are curtailed, or when fewer scholarships are provided for local residents. And when universities are pressured to achieve, where their students are concerned, not equality of *opportunity* but equality of result—and *hang* the cost! Then no one should be shocked to discover how many of those on the school's payroll get *financially hanged* as a result.

What we take for granted in the corporate sector, when it comes to matters of income and expenditure, is what we must learn to take for granted where schools of higher education are concerned. All that I've said so far offers examples only of the ways in which traditional modes of academic governance and management are failing to keep pace with societal and economic developments that leap up at us from every newspaper and magazine, and crowd in upon us through our own observations. We live, after all, in the age of Pat Buchanan, a rhetorician whose mind and tongue work at the speed of light even when he is articulating points of view that many find erroneous or positively grotesque. But if Buchanan, or some successor to Buchanan, eventually succumbs to temptation and launches a full-fledged anti-academic campaign—of the sort Buchanan himself has already nibbled at—can anyone doubt that he will draw admirers from those who find that his quickness of mind and fast pace offer a hilarious contrast to the slow motion, the ponderous, committee-paced uncertainty, of his academic antagonists?

And does the history of our century suggest that we are wisest to simply ignore the threat offered by demagogues with a fingertip "feel" for what the desperate citizens in their audiences long to hear? And have we *absolutely* seen the last of the phenomenon described by the late Richard Hofstadter, namely anti-intellectualism in American political life?

One of the conclusions I am prepared to reach at *this* point is that never in my adult life have American schools of higher education looked as *vulnerable* as they do today, especially when we recall the extent to which they serve projective and fantasy functions for so many Americans. Their fixed costs are high, and getting ever higher, as can be confirmed by this year's quotes for the medical insurance policies that will cover university employees in 1992-93. Meanwhile, the amounts they can charge for their services are far more constrained than was the case only a few years ago, and, regardless of need, can only be raised much more slowly.

Moreover, recent "*scandals*" have carved deep wounds in their public status, most of all the scandals involving so-called "research overhead costs" billed to government agencies. And the unending disputes over curriculum and over both student and faculty demographics have left behind, fairly or unfairly, the sense of American higher education as preoccupied with everything *except* education, and of individual schools as (a) not in full control of what they are doing, and (b) not fully certain about what they *ought* to be doing.

I haven't spared the black paint in portraying our present academic typhoon, and so I really must apologize for adding a bit more of it to my canvas. I cannot conclude without at least a brief discussion of the phenomenon called *tenure*.

I needn't tell you what a great forward step tenure represented when, in the late 1930s and early 1940s, it was introduced into American academic life. Today, we rub our eyes in disbelief at some of the tales out of the earlier twentieth century, when even a figure like Charles Beard could be hounded, threatened and subjected to a variety of indignities by the president of his university, and when the very *idea* of "academic freedom" could still draw puzzled looks from trustees and administrators in higher education.

It was tenure that enabled American schools of higher education to rise to their high status as centers of research, models of undergraduate education, and magnets for students from every part of the world. It made certain that arbitrary political roadblocks could no longer be flung across the pathways of knowledge and the processes of free, wide-ranging academic discourse.

Where the institution of tenure is concerned, that day is long gone. Even moderate critics of higher education are no longer a surprise when they question whether "academic freedom" has gone far too far, and is now the cloak regularly donned by tenured practitioners of pure outrage. Meanwhile, even its most enthusiastic advocates no longer deny that the issue of tenure, today, is an issue centered around *job security*.

What we are witnessing at the present moment, therefore, is a growing risk of head-on collision between the American academic world and what is becoming an increasingly anti-tenure American society. In our newly anxious and insecure country, where no one on a payroll any longer feels that his or her next paycheck is a guaranteed certainty, tenure can be described as *exactly* the institution calculated to "rub people the wrong way."

Among those who have already learned that bitter lesson are physicians, people who work in the civil service, including teachers in public elementary and secondary schools, and lawyers, all the way up to the partners of major law firms. We are hearing more and more about the need to severely restrict the number of terms served by federal and state legislators—the length, in short, of their legislative *tenures*—and the number of years served by corporate directors. In a related upheaval, once-powerful labor unions have discovered just how rabid average citizens now become when they hear about the kinds of work-rules that both labor and management once took for granted, the kind that could be seen as nothing but *make-work* alias salaried retirement alias positions protected by *tenure*.

At the opposite extreme from tenure is America's most important buzzword of the 1980s and 1990s: *accountability*. And what that translates into is the ability of both salaried individuals and the organizations that employ them to deliver, if necessary at the drop of a hat, a full and fully satisfactory explanation of what they have actually done to justify amounts of money received and amounts of money expended.

Yes, this brave new world is a far grimmer one than even academic pessimists could envision only 10 or 15 years ago. Yes, it is infinitely less humane than the one that so recently prevailed, *even* in the early "Reagan Years." Yes, it tends toward ruthless quantification of the sort that simply "cuts across the grain" of so many academic realities. And yes, it is positively addicted to the postlapsarian vision notion that only "a *new* broom sweeps clean," and that people not under continuous scrutiny will almost inevitably succumb to corruption.

But what is more important is that in trying to maintain an earlier academic order *built* upon the institution of tenure, our schools of higher education risk what I have already called a head-on collision with the society that ultimately supports them—without whose support they would simply vanish, like the monasteries disestablished by Henry the Eighth, and be replaced with some entirely new ways of accomplishing the same goals.

I began with the fable of a frog mystified by his transformation from the status of prince. I would like to end on a somewhat hopeful note. What those who teach in and who administer our schools of higher education must accomplish right now is an act of creative adaptation on a truly massive scale. They must convince the rest of American society *not* to scapegoat them for matters far beyond their control. But in order to stand a chance of accomplishing that, they must *not* offer easy targets to the political marksmen now being flung up by the troubled American economy. By "giving a little *here*" they will find themselves "getting a little *there*." For politics, like a *limited financial system*, is very much a matter of trade-offs.

What will be required of academicians in the years immediately before us are qualities like flexibility and imagination and openness of mind—qualities not necessarily taught in graduate schools but qualities infallibly taught by life. If those on our campuses can only look beyond campus walls, if they can only see themselves as *other* Americans see them, then their Fairy Godmother will infallibly put in an appearance, bestow her kiss on their froggy lips, and lo! The prince will be back again!

CAN POLITICAL CORRECTNESS EVER BE POLITICALLY INCORRECT?

"P.C." *has become* a crucial piece of ammunition in the armory of those in American life, including state legislators and federal politicians, who would like to launch a wholesale assault against colleges and universities, who would like to "expose" the working-habits and intellectual standards of both professors and administrators, and who would like, where schools of higher education are concerned, to "cut them down to size" by first cutting their *budgets* down to size.

State and federal politicians are so eager to use "p.c." in this fashion, as the cutting-edge of their guillotine, because they sense that such a step will meet with a good deal of public approval.

That's how thoroughly and how successfully the mere *mention* of "p.c." sets American teeth on edge. *That's* how most Americans in their thirties, forties and fifties feel when they hear, of course, titles which imply that the *Iliad*, the *Odyssey*, *Hamlet* and *War and Peace* are all the work of dead, white, reactionary males—and that they deserve no more automatic reverence than a novel published two years ago or a play currently undergoing its first performance, especially when the authors of that novel and that play are black, Hispanic or Native American.

So the very first thing I'd like to do is amend my title somewhat, and have it read: "Can the Political Poison Called 'P.C.' Ever Be Rendered Less Poisonous?" And I'd also like to add a *sub*title, whose meaning I'll make clear: *"What's All This Political Stuff About Anyway?"*

How did "p.c." get started? And why has it spread sufficiently far and wide to be threatening the very future of our schools of higher education?

For an answer to that question, I'll go all the way back to my own college education, which took place at Columbia between 1955 and 1959. One thing was for sure about Columbia: *a number* of its students during those years, and *some of those* who set its essential tone, were from New York, Jewish, immigrant backgrounds of the type we would today characterize as "upwardly mobile." Another thing was for sure about Columbia—this demographic fact was nowhere, but *nowhere*, acknowledged in the college's undergraduate curriculum.

The curriculum consisted of works drawn from the Western Tradition, which, we were told more often implicitly than explicitly, ran from the ancient Greeks to the Christian Middle Ages, soaking up the Old Testament along the way, and from there to such modern figures as Nietzsche, T. S. Eliot, D.H. Lawrence and William Butler Yeats—figures who were either steeped in nostalgia for the Middle Ages and/or anti-Semitic and/or in violent reaction against the Christianity of their childhoods.

And where that left us as students was a bit of a mystery. Many of us got excellent grades that helped to launch us into splendid careers by mastering the Western Christian Tradition more thoroughly than any Western or Eastern Christian had ever even pretended to do. But anyone who expressed even a modest interest in looking at human history and civilization from a *Jewish* point of view was pointed firmly uptown, toward the Jewish Theological Seminary, and told to go and take a couple of courses *there*. In short, our Judaism—if we felt it at all—was okay *in its place*, and that place was definitely *not* Columbia College.

Only compare this state of affairs with the one that now exists at every major university in the United States. A department or division or school of Jewish Studies, covering Jewish history and literature and culture, is *of course* an essential part of the curriculum at those schools. And students who don't care to immerse themselves in Augustine's *City of God* or the *Divine Comedy* of Dante or the works of Saint Thomas Aquinas feel perfectly comfortable about going to that department or division or school of Jewish Studies in order to take courses on Hebrew poetry of the Middle Ages, the history of Zionism and the State of Israel, the Holocaust, and the sociology of American Judaism.

I hope I'm not committing a major act of blasphemy when I say that what happened in the years following my graduation from

Columbia was that making room in the undergraduate curriculum for Jewish Studies became the *politically correct* thing to do. All of a sudden, the obvious importance of the Western Christian Tradition for each of our lives and for our collective *way* of life was a lot less obvious. Suddenly, the notion that Western history and civilization could be looked at from *other* points of view, including the points of view of those Jews and Muslims, Asians and others whom the Christian West had relentlessly persecuted, was as obvious as the fact that grass is green and the sky, when not overcast, blue.

Similar developments marked the academic curriculum in parts of the United States with significant Italian-American, Polish-American or other "ethnic" populations. Groups like these, though historically Christian, began to see their own histories and cultures as set apart, to some degree, from the line of so-called "high culture" that ran from Greco-Roman antiquity to the Renaissance, and from there through the culture of Northern Europe in the nineteenth and twentieth centuries.

But the effect of these various academic movements and programs, with their typical emphasis on modern rather than ancient literature, was minimal compared to the emergence of Afro-American Studies, followed by the emergence of other academic programs devoted to studying groups from non-European and/or non-Western backgrounds. To those of my own collegiate generation—those who came of intellectual age in the period from the end of the Second World War to the early 1960s—the notion that we could cut the basic curriculum *entirely* loose from Judeo-Christian roots, including not only the Greco-Roman classics but also the Bible, came as a profound shock.

And that shock has, if anything, intensified in more recent years, as the rejection of historically Western values has blended into the broader pattern of what is now known as "p.c." What has happened, in effect, is that a proposed restructuring or *destructuring* of cultural values, based on the notion of our world as one of *multiple* traditions, has combined with the inheritance, from the Sixties and early Seventies, of what was then known as the "counter-culture." And what the "counter-culture" maintained back then, that Europe and America represented a society given to paternalism, racism, colonialism and the destruction of the natural environment, has become a mainstream in the pattern of thinking—or more often, *feeling*—now associated with "political correctness."

So well-known has this pattern and this set of attitudes become, and such a favorite topic of the print and electronic media, that it seems to have been with us forever. It takes a moment of thought to remind ourselves that it has actually been with us, in its current form, for only a few years. And that is why we are only at the point of *beginning* to ask some obvious questions about it, such as:

- Why does "p.c." seem to have spread at such a wildfire pace?
- Why have college undergraduates proven so susceptible to it? And,
- Is it in fact a complete novelty, or does it—like the Western Tradition that formerly ruled the intellectual roost—have a tradition, and roots, of its own?

In seeking to answer those questions, I'd like to begin by making a relatively simple assertion. All of us know of the extent to which a society's adolescents function as *bellwethers*, cluing the rest of that society's members in with regard to that society's tensions, conflicts and future direction—the extent to which adolescents make an *obvious* display of themes that older citizens keep hidden, speak of in muffled or whispered fashion, or simply deny. Only in historical retrospect does it become obvious that those seeking clues about the future would have been wiser to look at their own 16-year-olds than at the latest utterances of the world's presidents and prime ministers.

Well, I see no reason why that general historical rule should have been suspended in *our* case. The college-age adolescents who are drawn to or are immersed in the values of "political correctness" are at some level functioning as spokespersons for the *rest* of us. And what they seem to be saying, in that classical role of bellwether, is, among other things:

- That *we* have lost confidence in our own tradition, even though we were imbued with it less than half a century ago.
- That *we* are having a lot of difficulty reconciling ourselves to the rapidly altering ethnic and socioeconomic patterns of our own society. And,

- That *we* are having particularly grave problems in accepting the notion that the predominance of our tradition was connected with the predominance of our economic and military strength, which is now in such steep decline.

We aren't going to cope with the "p.c." phenomenon until we acknowledge its fundamental rightness on one major issue: that for several hundred years, Western nations achieved and maintained their global hegemony by employing the talents of their citizens who had graduated from Oxford, Cambridge, the Sorbonne, Harvard, Yale, Princeton and other bastions of the Western Tradition—a tradition whose cultural core was based mainly on works originally written in Greek and Latin, and then, in the more recent "humanities" curriculum, on works originally written in all of the languages of Western Europe. And that those graduates did their work with the support of technologically advanced weapons and major colonial armies.

The Jewish students with whom I went to college could "hook on" to this tradition, so to speak, because their backgrounds were European and because their scriptures *did* play a central role in defining the Christian culture of the West. Students from *other* European backgrounds—the so-called "ethnics"—could also, if they wished, find aspects of the Western tradition with which to identify. Italian-Americans had Dante, so to speak, while Irish-Americans had Yeats.

But what neither they nor their WASP contemporaries could have imagined was a period like the present, when America's so-called racial and linguistic "minorities," black, Hispanic and Asian, would begin to form a *majority* of the American population, a significant percentage of college and university students, and increasingly influential voices in the determination of the academic curriculum.

Nor could either students or faculty, in those early postwar years, have imagined an American society in which younger people of all social, racial and ethnic backgrounds would be so immersed in computers and the electronic media as they are today, so much a part of a world driven by "instant information," that they would find the lengthier works of the traditional curriculum, including the works of Homer, Virgil, Dante, Milton and most of the eighteenth-and nineteenth-century novelists, almost impossible to "get through."

There is a sense in which American colleges and universities have never had a choice. They have *always* had to appeal to the young people actually being turned out by American society. At a time when their students were mainly of white, Anglo-Saxon and Protestant derivation, and came, so to speak, from "Shakespeare-reading families," they taught Shakespeare, *and* Augustine, *and* Dante, *and* Milton, *and* the major Western writers of the eighteenth and nineteenth centuries.

As the years went by, and the experience of the World War I etched its way into the younger generation's minds, colleges and universities gradually added to their curriculum such previously tabu writers as Nietzsche, T. S. Eliot, D. H. Lawrence and James Joyce. In the years following World War II, even Norman Mailer, Arthur Miller, Saul Bellow, William Golding and Herbert Marcuse found their way into the curriculum, because only in this way could the curriculum be conveyed to young people with a greatly diminished reverence for their ostensible civilization.

But even with all of this stretching, the curriculum was still, fundamentally, Western, because that was still the orientation of a large majority of the students attending, and therefore defining, our schools of higher education.

Now we are confronted with an altogether new phenomenon: the need to appeal to, and therefore gain access to the minds of, students whose backgrounds include no automatic allegiances to Western literary and artistic traditions, including those that represent utmost modernity, or perhaps no apparent allegiances of this kind. And that is where the academic mainstream needs to learn some lessons from those who presently espouse points of view that seem imbued with "political correctness."

What the mainstream needs to drop, obviously, are the subtle and sometimes not-so-subtle hints that "p.c." is synonymous with anti-Westernism, anti-Europeanism, and sometimes even anti-semitism, because that makes "political correctness" a matter of *them* rather than *us*. At the same time, what the mainstream needs to *avoid* is the complacent sense that a "return to older values" is all that's needed to put our humanistic Humpty-Dumpty together again. If today's upper-middle-income and upper-income students from affluent suburbs are a lot less verbal, a lot more visual, and a lot more electronically "tuned in" than *we* were at their age, then the mandate to redesign our curricula isn't coming *just* from American minority-groups. Rather, such redesign is a requirement for dealing with the vast majority of today's and tomorrow's students, regardless of their precise social and ethnic backgrounds.

Now I am going to propose to you something that will sound truly heretical, and something I would definitely *not* have suggested as recently as five years ago, which is that the clue to a redefined curriculum is to be found in a redesigned pedagogical *style*—one that makes adroit and sensitive use of the full range of computerized technology now available for teaching purposes.

To demonstrate exactly what I mean, let me paint you what I hope will be a living and dynamic portrait. In a lecture hall sit 50 freshman students, drawn from a variety of backgrounds. Each has before him or her a personal computer attached to a laser printer. Behind the instructor is a very large screen, clearly visible even to the students in the back row. The subject under discussion in *this* section of Global Civilization 101 is ancient Egypt and its relationship to all of the ethnic groups of the ancient Mediterranean world.

The students have been introduced in a previous class to the Egyptian dynasties from the Old Kingdom all the way down to the time of Alexander the Great, as well as their artistic and military accomplishments. The instructor now begins by flashing onto the screen a list of the major ethnic groups with whom the Egyptians made contact in this period of more than 3,000 years—a list that is automatically provided to each student by his or her laser printer. It includes Canaanites, usually referred to as "Syrians"; Phoenicians; Babylonians; Hittites; Assyrians; Nubians; Libyans; Persians; and, finally, Greeks. It also makes reference to the vision of Egypt in Hebrew tradition, as recorded in the earliest books of the Hebrew Bible.

As each of these groups is discussed by the instructor, appropriate materials are flashed onto the big screen—especially the very precise portraits of each of these ethnic groups that were created by Egyptian artists—and these materials are printed out at each student's desk for individual use. Soon it is time for the first individual exercise. Each student is asked to select one of the ethnic groups just covered by the instructor. Pushing a single button on the personal computer gives him or her a selective bibliography on the group chosen, consisting of a dozen or so articles, plus some sections from full-length books, and including material on art, architecture and handicrafts.

In one hour, each student must compose a brief, literate and grammatical summary—what the French would call a "précis"—that draws upon these materials in as comprehensive a fashion as possible. The summary is then "handed in" by the push of another button. And while these summaries are being read and annotated by the instructor's two graduate assistants, the instructor moves on to discuss the fateful clash of the Egyptian and Persian empires, leading to the ultimate conquest of Egypt by the Persians and the destruction of many of its monuments. In this way, the instructor, among other things, begins to prepare the students for the even more dramatic clash between the Persians and the *Greeks*, which ended with the conquest of the Persian Empire by Alexander.

Before the students leave, each, at his or her desk, receives the individual paper he or she did a few minutes earlier, with the comments and corrections of the teaching assistants. And all are given a homework assignment of some sort—perhaps a piece of reading that the computer, in one final burst of activity, prints out. And so much for libraries and the complaint that "there were no more copies on the shelf!"

Incidentally, all of us can be forgiven for "*knowing*" which student would choose which ethnic group. *Of course* the black students in the class would choose to examine Egypt's relationship with the Nubians from their African south, with whom the Egyptians fought countless battles, and by whom they were even, at one point, ruled. And *of course* the Jewish students would choose to discuss the portrait of Egypt that emerges from the books of Genesis and Exodus. And *of course* the students from various Middle Eastern backgrounds would focus in on the Persians or the Phoenicians or the Canaanites.

Maybe. But maybe not. The point about computerized information systems is how much information they offer, and how quickly one can move through it and select what's of interest. A student who starts in on the "obvious" choice can—even within the space of one hour—decide that it's too much of what he or she already knows, and that a switch to a different ethnic group is what he or she really wants.

In constructing this classroom scenario, I have deliberately kept myself within the borders of the traditional Western curriculum. But a comparable computer-based orchestration can be applied to an infinite number of other subjects, drawn from every world culture, from every part of the globe, and from every stage of world history. It can be applied to the history of American race relations, to World War II as seen from the vantage-point of Turkey or Australia or Latin America, to the Mongol conquests and their impact on both Europe and China, or to the birth-control policies pursued by every nation of the world at the present time.

And yes, let me agree with those who think that pedagogy of this kind will require new types of *pedagogues*, who move comfortably between traditional scholarship and contemporary information technology. Getting such teachers trained will be an important task in the years ahead, but not an insuperable one, given the fact that our younger scholars come from the same world of electronically available information as those who will soon be their students.

And only in this way, it seems to me, can we go about teaching— which means *attracting*—the young men and women, from every conceivable social, economic and ethnic background, whom we are now trying to educate.

I began by redoing its original title and asking whether "political correctness" could ever be rendered less poisonous to schools of higher education than it is presently proving. I moved on to my sense that the curricular conflicts on campuses mirror, in their political passions, the bleak politics of our divided nation and its shared sense of terminal despair.

I've now tried to offer my vision of a new type of education, one whose reach and whose appeal would be truly global, and one that would draw, in the most deliberate fashion, on the electronic and visual technologies that have captivated, are captivating, and will continue to captivate the minds of our young. In the process of doing this, I've tried to suggest that "politically correct" outlooks aren't to be wholly accepted or wholly rejected but to be *learned from*.

And I'd like to conclude by noting that why, in my opinion, this learning process, and the new mode of teaching that will spring from it, is so important.

It's so important because of the extent to which campus rebels against the domination of Western Culture are *themselves* dominated by Western Culture, which is the most self-critical culture the world has ever seen, and which has in fact taught them many of the most important arguments that they are now engaged in deploying against it.

From the Hebrew prophets to several Renaissance writers, and from them to modern novelists like E. M. Forster, D. H. Lawrence and George Orwell, Western literature has consisted to a remarkable extent of self-denunciations based on Western corruption, hypocrisy, callousness, racism and imperialism. And this tradition of rigorous self-scrutiny, this demand for high standards that are actually adhered to *even* under stress, is the most important legacy schools of higher education can transmit to their students.

Colleges and universities, in other words, have been created—and have created themselves—in order to *embody* this tradition of self-scrutiny. If it *does* get transmitted, and if our graduates *are* able to apply it to their own lives and adult functions, then there is hope for the future of American society and its role in our ever more interdependent world. If it *doesn't* get transmitted, and if graduates go on to lives driven by short-term "input" and an absence of rigorous reasoning, then the American decline that so many of us fear is upon us will in fact turn out to be not the wave but the trough of our collective future.

Our young people are the key. If we recapture their imaginations, if we inspire them with our ideals, then in the process of giving *them* hope we will know there is hope for *us*. And at that point we will look back and say: " 'Political correctness' was ever so politically *in*-correct. But, praise God, it enabled us to correct *our*selves."

1993

Quality Management
How Do You Make It Total?

Like most people whose careers have undergone several decades of development, I have become a connoisseur of both compliments and criticisms. Those I've *recently* received are stacked in a kind of wine-cellar inside my head. I make my way through it, pulling down this or that bottle, blowing away the dust and the cobwebs, checking the precise vintage . . . and then I relive its flavor, its bouquet, and perhaps—*if* it's a compliment, and *if* it's a compliment of the very finest sort—the delicious afterglow that continued to thrill my palate and the upper part of my digestive tract for many minutes after I took my first exploratory sip.

Right now, the bottle that thrills me most is a relatively young vintage bottled by the Society for College and University Planning . . . *so* young that there isn't any dust on it at all. It was less than a year ago, after all, that I addressed the 27th Annual Conference of the S.C.U.P. on the subject of the new planning environment with which our schools of higher education are *currently* struggling to cope. Only a few months then elapsed, and presto! I was invited to speak to you today at the annual conference of the Mid-Atlantic Region. Among the precious bottles on the *complimentary* side of my internal wine-cellar, *this* one represents a vintage I truly prize, and have already shared with my nearest and dearest!

As I was winding up the talk I gave in Minneapolis last August, I found myself drawn into the kind of language and the kind of thinking that is often identified, today, with Total Quality Management and its "customer orientation."

"The challenges now facing each and every college and university," I declared, "mandates participation by all concerned. So competitive have our schools of higher education become—so desperate, in many cases, for additional students—that every person on the school payroll needs to do his or her darndest just to keep enrollments stable. Students and their families must be treated with levels of respect that could barely have been conceived of 10 years ago . . . must be treated, in effect, as valued customers rather than obvious and expected clients. Suddenly, the job of every faculty member, administrator and staff-person looks tough and demanding, with quick responses and sharp analytic capacities as premium qualities. Suddenly, the need for business-like thinking is no longer confined to the Business Office, but has begun to pervade every part of the academic organization."

And what I might have added in Minneapolis was that *suddenly* these very sharp and analytic capacities must be used *on behalf* of rather than *within* the organization—the school—that pays one's salary. *Suddenly* they must be deployed in a distinctly cooperative rather than a critical fashion. And *suddenly*, the motto inscribed over the gateway that leads to the Halls of Ivy must read "WE'RE ALL IN THIS TO-GETHER" rather than "EVERY MAN AND WOMAN FOR HIM-SELF OR HERSELF."

Just between you and me: that's *amazing*. Here we are, after all, in one of the most competitive societies our planet has ever spawned—a society whose members are all the more competitive because it is so profoundly democratic, and so *dis*inclined toward any form of truly hereditary privilege—and suddenly we are being told to go against our culture and our instincts, and to internalize a new ethic altogether: the notion that each member of the organization can help to make it more competitive—and his or her paycheck more secure—by deploying his or her intelligence, his or her analytic strength, and his or her imaginative powers in a *cooperative* manner . . . one, more-over, that puts a special premium on the capacity for *self*-criticism and the kind of "personal job awareness" that amounts to continuous self-monitoring.

No wonder W. Edwards Deming, when he first came up with the idea of Total Quality Management, found almost no takers in this country, and was greeted with enthusiasm in the nation of Japan, where cooperation was a historic value instilled in each citizen from infancy and early childhood on. No wonder it is the Japanese whose highest industrial honor is still called the Deming Award. And no wonder it wasn't until 1989, four years ago, that the Japanese Union of Scientists and Engineers first bestowed the Deming Award on an American company, Florida Power and Light.

And in order to outline the relevance of Florida Power and Light's experience to the academic world in which we find ourselves today, I'm going to quote just a few sentences from a book by Alexander Hiam that was published last year and that represents the most up-to-date thinking of the conference board, an international network of major companies and executives often quoted on the business pages of our newspapers and magazines. The book is entitled *Closing the Quality Gap: Lessons from America's Leading Companies,* and the description of the Florida Power and Light experience is from a chapter called "Planning for Quality."

"FPL's quality journey began in 1981," Hiam writes, "just two years after the Three Mile Island accident had attracted the nation's attention to quality issues at electric utilities. It reflected a recognition that 'The company's internal and external environments were changing faster than the organization could adapt and that corporate goals needed to be established and achieved using new management techniques.' "

FPL chairman Marshall McDonald puts it more colorfully:

"I made the observation that we had been looking at the horse from the wrong end, and it was not a pretty sight. We had been concerned with keeping rejects down, instead of quality up. We had been busy keeping imperfection under control rather than trying for perfection. We had sometimes burnt the toast and then scraped it clear, instead of fixing the toaster. Some of us had even learned to like burnt toast."

Hiam goes on to describe in some detail the quality improvement process that Florida Power and Light created in the mid-1980s. Its three components are policy deployment, quality in daily work, and quality improvement teams. And the really crucial part is that policy deployment, which sets long-term, short-term and mid-term plans for FPL, is based on a system of *consensus-based decision-making.* "Senior management can no longer define the specific strategies that will accomplish corporate goals," Hiam writes, "the hands-on analysis of individual processes by the people who know them best is required"—and the primary documents with which those hands-on people work are consumer surveys.

The critical sentence generated by Florida Power and Light, and quoted by Hiam, is one that I myself will quote to you once again. What FPL recognized was that "the company's internal and external environments were changing faster than the organization could adapt *and that corporate goals needed to be established and achieved using new management techniques.*" Is there a better description of the challenges that now confront America's colleges and universities? It sometimes feels as if there is not a single aspect of the functioning they took for granted a few years ago that is not being subjected—right now—to a sustained critical bombardment.

And as for burning the toast and scraping it clear, or getting used to burned toast, only take as an example what until recently was considered an average administrative scenario. At College or University X, a parent telephones in order to question an item that has appeared on the most recent tuition bill. The parent is told, none too politely, that he or she has reached the wrong office, and should have dialled Extension 2653. "I'd try transferring you," says the employee, "but the phones never work right and I'm too busy right now so please dial again." The employee hangs up without bothering to learn that while College or University X is located in Pennsylvania, the parent is calling from Honolulu. And the parent, after getting a busy-signal for a quarter of an hour, finally discovers that Extension 2653 connects him or her directly to the Office of Campus Maintenance.

Need I tell you what so often came next—and on whose desk the burned toast ended up? The president of the university, in between 10 million other commitments and crises, had to deal with an outraged letter from Honolulu. "My daughter is a student in your *business school,*" the letter might say, "and you appear to be running your own school in a *totally unbusiness-like fashion.* I'm going to advise her to seek an academic environment that *practices what it preaches.*"

That was the bad old world—the customer-relations snakepit—out of which our schools of higher education are seeking to raise themselves. What more and more of them are trying to do, through their TQM programs, is to change the entire *culture* of the academy to see to it that every employee from the president to the most recently hired member of the maintenance staff thinks in a holistic manner about his or her job and its relation to the well-being, and the fiscal health, of the entire school.

Now, *culture* is an old, old world where academicians are concerned. University-based anthropologists have been making use of it for most of the twentieth century. Professors of English know that one of the most famous works of Matthew Arnold, the nineteenth-century British author, was entitled *Culture and Anarchy.* And it's all the more surprising, therefore, that in today's day and age it is the *corporate* sector of the economy that's much further along, when it comes to discussions of internal organizational culture, than the higher education sector.

In the book by Alexander Hiam that I've already cited, for example, a separate highlighted section is devoted to the subject of "Creating a Quality Culture." Corporate culture, Hiam writes,

> is reflected in the relationships among employees, the mores and taboos within a company, the legends and stories told, even the language and imagery used when discussing business decisions. It can be transmitted through subtle messages such as the way parking spaces or offices are allocated or the nicknames applied to managers when they are not listening.
>
> It can also be manifested in more obvious ways, such as in the criteria by which advancements and raises are awarded. Culture is a subtle but tremendously powerful influence over everything people do. It can influence not only employees but also suppliers, distributors and others within its reach.

And now I ask you: What is the main challenge that arises when we try to apply this same kind of thinking to an academic as opposed to a business situation?

The main challenge, I believe, has to do with the existence, at a school of higher education, of a rather important group of people known as *faculty members.* It is around *their* work, *their* needs, and above all *their* students that the college or university as a whole quite properly revolves. And what is particularly important and significant in this context is that they represent a group of people who by and large don't think of themselves as or like to be referred to as *employees*.

What this translates into is that in the academic setting, the effort to achieve Total Quality Management has to take careful account of the ways in which faculty members, as opposed to all the other people on the school payroll, are *socialized*, as well as the ways in which they influence the thinking and feeling of everybody else on the institutional payroll. Among the most important points that must be explored are:

1. The kinds of people who *self-select*—at some point in their teens or twenties—and begin to think of a professorial career as appropriate for *them*.

2. The ethics, values, procedures and psychological tonalities through which they pass as they go about earning the appropriate professorial credentials.

3. The types of functioning that then come to be considered normative, by them and their academic peers, once they are working full time in a college or university.

4. The impact that those types of functioning have on all of the other workers who draw their salaries from the school budget.

I don't think I'm saying anything radical or even controversial when I observe that those who are most inclined to choose an academic career tend to be *more verbally inclined* than the average American, more given to criticism and to the need for *proof*, and far less likely to accept a pleasing appearance as the substitute for a documentable reality.

Professors bear some distinct resemblances to lawyers, in other words. But whereas a lawyer knows that all of these inclinations must be harnessed to the need to win cases, which in turn means you win more clients, which in turn means you win a higher salary, the professor is arguably yoked to an ideal of absolute truth regardless of truth's practical consequences. That is why professors have so often felt justified in joining student picket-lines outside the administration building or in denouncing their school's policies in front of reporters and television cameras.

The culture that faculty members generate when they gather together in an academic setting is therefore one that is rather unique. And what I mean by that is that while they transact certain obvious administrative necessities during their professional lives—everything implied by departments, by votes, by chairpersons, by deans and by vice-presidents—many don't see those parts of their lives as central to their *real identities*.

In between their first inclinations toward higher education and their first full-time job, future professors are shaped by their graduate training. And within that training, they are typically subjected to processes of testing and challenge—summed up by the dissertation defense—that can impact on them in isolating ways.

This is followed by a reinforcing process that begins once they are on the full-time payroll of a college or university. They *know*, at that point, that nothing will advance their careers more quickly and effectively than a nationwide reputation within their individual disciplines. Indeed, the metaphors that dominate their thinking about themselves, once they have become fully committed to an academic career, are *independent* rather than *organizational*, and *heroic* rather than *cooperative*.

And sometimes these tendencies are further enhanced when a faculty member is an excellent teacher—otherwise known as a "star performer," the kind of person who "gets students to sit up and take notice." It's no wonder that angry college or university presidents, when they aren't being overheard by outsiders, are likely to complain that dealing with their faculty is like "dealing with a bunch of primadonnas" or "trying to herd cats."

But complaints like that seem to me to miss the point. The unanswered question in American higher education today is whether the faculty members who represent the heart of our schools of higher education, as a result of all of these influences, shaping experiences and reinforcements, represent a *culture*— an entire way of doing things—that is compatible or incompatible with the goals of Total Quality Management. And the secondary question that immediately follows is whether they also represent a culture that is harmonious with or permanently alienated from the culture of all the *other* people on the college or university payroll.

All over the United States, TQM programs have gotten underway in the academic setting. With certain notable exceptions, they can be described—to use the adjective an administrator at my university recently applied to our *own* TQM process—as "embryonic." My own sense is that they are being implemented far more swiftly where college and university staff members—especially those working in non-academic areas—are concerned, than in anything having directly to do with those who teach and/or do research and/or do academic "outreach" work with the surrounding community.

I return to a once-famous book in which a British writer, C. P. Snow, concerned about the gap that seemed to separate the humanities and the physical sciences, asked whether the intellectual life of his time was being marked by the emergence of "two cultures"—two cultures that could not really communicate with each other.

The great risk now being run by our schools of higher education is the possibility that they are turning themselves into doughnuts or bagels. Through Total Quality Management, the periphery will be shaped up—but in the center, where the faculty members live, there will be what amounts to an attitudinal hole . . . cosmetically disguised, no doubt, but effectively non-functional.

Put yourself in the shoes of a senior faculty member whose socialization, as an academic, took place in the 1950s or the early 1960s. He or she completed the Ph.D. and became a professor at a time when students were flocking into our colleges and when money was no problem. He or she has always taken pride in publication, in papers delivered at professional conferences, and in being a tough and demanding teacher whose less ambitious students would transfer to another section of the same course.

Now, he or she is being asked to think of students and their families as *customers*, to carefully monitor their satisfaction or dissatisfaction with the professor's services, and to be quite open about the fact that he or she may need some outside assistance—some retraining, even—if he or she is to become a productive member of the school payroll from a TQM point of view. As a *senior* faculty member, moreover, this professor is being asked to sit with his or her colleagues in order to discuss, regularly and at length, "quality improvement" in the department as a whole.

To an extent that senior administrators sometimes fail to appreciate, faculty members *do* set the tone and *do* powerfully contribute to the culture of a college or university. The institution of tenure, by its guarantee of longevity, makes them all the more influential in that respect. And right now, the future of Total Quality Management in the higher education sector hinges on whether they can be drawn into its presuppositions and procedures. What seems most unlikely is that a successful "quality improvement culture" can be developed within a school of higher learning whose full-time faculty remain permanently separate from it.

A similar question-mark hangs over the role that TQM can or cannot play in the work-lives of part-time teachers and teaching assistants, who make up a growing percentage of the instructors on university payrolls. TQM is a time-consuming process. What these folks have the very *least* of is, as you all know, time. (Money, I suspect, runs a close second.)

The tight and scary American economy of the present and immediate future, I should add, cuts two ways where academicians are concerned. On the one hand, many professors are becoming distinctly more inclined toward cooperative and communal functioning because they realize they can count themselves lucky if their job is stable, their paycheck predictable, and their school in reasonable shape. On the other hand, heightened competitiveness in the academic world— *between* colleges and *between* those seeking promotion and/or tenure— can reinforce some of the isolating and independent thought-patterns that I've already discussed today.

For college and university planners, these questions are far more than—if you'll forgive me—academic. They are questions about the very medium in which you do your work. What your individual and collective futures will be like . . . *that* will depend, in the long term, on the most fundamental principle of quality management—that it's either total or it's nothing.

~~~~~~~~

REMARKS, THE D.C. JEWISH COMMUNITY CENTER'S
JOHN R. RISHER PUBLIC AFFAIRS FORUM
MAY 6, 1993, WASHINGTON, D.C.

THE FUTURE OF HIGHER EDUCATION

This title assumes that American higher education has a future. That's no longer a point of view to be taken for granted. For several years now, our colleges and universities have been enjoying, or more accurately, *not* enjoying, what's generally known as a "bad press." Whole books have been published to tell us that professors are shirking their duties, that administrators are mainly concerned to hire more administrators, and that financial scandal—once a specialty of Wall Street—is now quite at home in the Halls of Ivy.

Putting myself in *your* shoes—asking myself what higher education must look like to members of the lay public who read *The Washington Post*, *The Wall Street Journal*, the major newsmagazines, and perhaps *The New York Times*—I frankly feel a touch of discouragement. Boy! Things *really* aren't looking good!

Then I step back a bit and take a good look at my own school, The George Washington University—I try to rise above the rosy glow of GW's recent basketball triumphs—and I'm amazed, as I focus in on its purely academic end, at how little of this grand critique of the last few years actually applies to this one specific institution. As nearly as I can make out from my rather intense observations, GW professors are *very* concerned about the educational experiences of their students, GW administrators are working longer and longer hours as they seek to make their parts of the school as efficient and as cost-effective as possible . . . there are no financial-mismanagement charges being thrown at GW by either governmental or private plaintiffs . . . and though the school is by no means perfect, those on its payroll are now engaged in a systematic effort at self-reform. One of the main aspects of that effort is our Total Quality Management program— which doesn't differ, in any significant way, from the TQM programs that are revolutionizing so much of American business and industry.

~~~~~~~~

Needless to say, I'm tempted by the idea that my university is the exception that proves the rule, and that if only all the *other* schools in the country would have the good sense to do things GW's way, then the future of American higher education would be assured. But I'm going to resist that temptation, and I'm going to start my comments today with a quick summary of what's *right* about our colleges and universities. I'll then move on to a discussion of what colleges and universities are now doing, from coast to coast, in order to expand their areas of *rightness* while carefully editing out the activities and behaviors that are *not* so good.

What's *right* about our schools of higher education can best be seen from a global perspective. American faculty members and administrators never cease to marvel at the sheer attractiveness of their institutions to students from abroad—young men and women who come here from Asia, from Europe, from Latin America, and from every other continent in order to obtain the skills and training they need for their careers. Indeed, this situation has now reached the point at which foreign students represent *such* a high percentage of those enrolled in our graduate schools of science, engineering and business that Americans are getting just a little bit nervous. Why is it, they ask, that America's primary and secondary education systems can't produce high achievers of this kind in anything like the same high numbers? What is it—at the elementary and secondary levels—that keeps young Americans from taking the same advantage of the finest universities our planet has ever produced?

But that's jumping ahead a bit, and right now I want to focus in on the fact that what we in this country take for granted when we think of a "college" or a "university" strikes the rest of the world as close to miraculous. In Europe, for example, in some of the most highly industrialized countries on our planet, higher education can represent a rather unattractive way of life—for both students and faculty. Classrooms are often overcrowded. Getting some books out of the library may take days of concentrated effort. Supportive facilities for students in academic or psychological trouble—the kinds of facilities we Americans take for granted—may be weak or nonexistent. Huge lecture classes—the kind that are always being protested against in the United States—may be the only classes there are.

And what's lacking in schools of higher education beyond our borders is, above all, the attitude, which our own colleges and universities do so much to promote and encourage, that a school of higher education exists to *serve* its students, to *help* them with their lives and their careers, and thereby to *support* the health and competitiveness of our national economy.

Even in their most intellectual strivings, in other words, American colleges and universities play certain kinds of *social* roles that have been assigned to them by our population as a whole—roles that sometimes cost a lot of money and that help to account for their rising tuition-levels. American schools of higher education, for example, are expected to be of special service to citizens from a variety of cultural, ethnic, racial, linguistic and economic backgrounds, as well as students with physical handicaps.

American colleges and universities are expected to play helpful roles for the communities in which they are located, especially if those are communities with serious social and economic problems. Our schools of higher education are also expected to provide authorities—people whom the media can reach over the telephone—on a whole variety of subjects ranging from medicine and foreign policy to religion and nuclear physics. And especially at a time like the present, they are expected to do the kinds of research that ultimately translate into new products, new industrial procedures, new medical treatments, and lots and lots of new jobs.

Last, but far from least, American schools of higher education are expected to provide, on a regional or national basis, centers of recreation and entertainment. Some of our citizens look to their football or basketball teams. Others attend a variety of exhibits, concerts, lectures and other cultural events. "Outreach" programs of various kinds bring whole areas of skill and knowledge to those willing to sign up for even a single course. Senior citizens often move to the vicinity of a large university precisely because it provides so many ways of passing the time, or learning to improve one's limited income, or finally receiving one's BA, MA or other higher degree.

In short, our colleges and universities are expected to be *totally involved* with their society—in ways that are simply *not* true of schools in other nations. And having gone a long way toward meeting those expectations, and toward being all things to all people, they now find themselves under challenge—from the American public—in ways that guarantee *some* major changes in what most of us have come to take for granted.

For example, and here we begin to move into the *future* of higher education, many of our colleges and universities are going to have to become more specialized places. For schools that calls themselves *universities*, that's a particular challenge—because it means that universal functioning is no longer possible for them. Difficult choices have to be made and are *being* made. That's why even major universities have started to phase out entire departments, schools and divisions—especially those whose enrollments are low and whose intellectual or practical value is dubious. That's why public universities with multiple campuses have begun to insist that duplications of function must be minimized—and that a student is often perfectly capable of traveling from Campus A to Campus B in order to obtain a particular kind of instruction. And that's why more and more colleges and universities, including some that rank as private rather than public schools of higher education, are exploring cooperative efforts of various kinds, including the sharing of certain expensive types of equipment.

As colleges and universities stop trying to be both utterly self-contained and boundlessly universal, those on their payrolls are having to measure up to some entirely new standards of accountability and productivity. The pressure for these new standards may come, at a private institution, from its board of trustees. At public colleges and universities, it may come from a state board of higher education or, as is the case today in Maryland, a state board of regents. Whatever the precise source of the pressure, though, it adds up to one thing: a requirement for the *quantification* of precisely *how much* is being spent on *what*, which includes the amount of benefit being received from those who get faculty salaries.

I hardly need to tell you that where American higher education is concerned, such demands for quantification go against the grain of a lot of historically established patterns and habits. As the Consortium for Policy Research in Education recently noted in its newsletter:

> Until recently, colleges and universities focused their efforts on obtaining increases in resources as a way to improve quality, not on finding better ways to use the resources already available to them.
>
> Now colleges and universities face new circumstances, including a much more critical attitude on the part of those who fund undergraduate education—parents, policymakers, the press and the general public. Institutions are being held accountable for the productive use of the resources they have, and appeals for extra funding fall on deaf ears.

And this is why truly wise schools of higher education *right now*, which I'm happy to say include my own university, aren't waiting for the bad news to arrive "from on high." They're moving into active programs of self-analysis and self-reform, looking at every corner of their operations in order to identify areas in need of reform—or areas and activities that can be radically cut back and sometimes eliminated altogether. The key to these self-analyses is most often a program of Total Quality Management—almost universally known, these days, by the acronym TQM.

It would be hard for me to overstate the totality that such a TQM effort represents. In effect, every single person on the school payroll is asked to adopt what for many represents an entirely new attitude. They are asked to re-envision themselves as *working partners* in the great cooperative effort that any school or business or government agency represents. They are asked to bring their critical faculties to bear on the work that they do, on the work that their entire office or department does, and on the relation that *their* work and their *department's* work has to the well-being and good functioning of the school as a whole.

Above all, those on the school payroll are asked to develop a sensitive and continuous "customer orientation." In the case of a college or university, that translates into a sharp awareness of the levels of service being delivered to students and their families—those, in short, who pay tuition. In a market that's become as tight and competitive as the market called higher education, there's simply no room for the older attitude that students are "just kids" of whom "there will always be more" and who "aren't going to be around long enough to complain."

Exactly the opposite attitude is what TQM programs strive for in higher education: that each and every student is a precious resource who, together with his or her family, sees to it that school income matches school expenditures and that yes, Virginia, there *will* be a pay-check coming at the end of *this* month, too!

As the newsletter I just quoted to you goes on to observe, though, productivity—including an emphasis on quality—is something that's relatively easy to define in business and industry but rather difficult to define in higher education. "But what does high quality mean in relation to the output of universities and colleges?" the newsletter asks. "Does it mean producing large amounts of useful research? Does it mean providing excellent teaching to undergraduates?"

That, in turn, leads us to realize just how important a school's *mission statement* has become in governing the self-assessment process that's so typically part of Total Quality Management. Mission statements were once regarded as mere glorified formalities—bits of noble verbiage to be printed at the front of the school catalogue. But in today's world, and as schools make those difficult decisions about their first, second and third priorities, even the *order* in which the mission statement lists the school's activities can serve as a guide to definitions of account-ability and productivity.

Suppose the statement declares that the mission of College or University X is "effective teaching that enhances the employability of our graduates, as well as the kinds of research whose value receives national and international recognition." Well, that implies quite a different agenda from the mission that is defined as "the advancement of knowl-edge in the natural sciences, the social sciences and the humanities, and the effective communication of such knowledge to our undergradu-ates and graduate students." In the first case, the school has licensed itself to promote a very cautious and selective research effort so that its primary energies can be focused on teaching. At the same time, it hasn't *ruled out* research, only, it hopes, the kinds of research that are definitely second-rate.

Meanwhile, the school that uses the second of these two mission statements has issued an implicit warning to potential undergraduates and their families: Don't enroll in *this* particular place if you're allergic to large lecture classes in which the lecturers are often teaching assistants, because world-class researchers, such as are typical of our faculty, seldom have the time or the energy to be of direct help to undergraduates.

In today's world, schools of higher education must *pick and choose* what they're going to do. Having picked and chosen, they can apply appropriate accountability standards, and appropriate productivity demands, to the work of their faculty members, their administrators and their staff.

So one of the things we can expect to see, as the future of higher education comes closer to being its present, is colleges and universities that—in comparison to those of even the recent past—look and feel a lot more businesslike. In addition to encouraging more businesslike attitudes among their faculty, administrators and staff, they will also be places that make much more pervasive and sophisticated use of electronic technology alias computers. At GW, for example, we have a new management information system that is well on the way to providing us with state-of-the-art capabilities in financial aid, student information, alumni affairs and development, human resources and finance. Improved software of this kind is also essential to the workings of an effective Total Quality Management program.

Since improvements of this kind tend to sound a bit soulless and mechanical, let me say right away that they are also revolutionizing the effectiveness of our colleges and universities where customer relations are concerned. The parent who calls in for some information about his or her child—information that may include questions about tuition owed, fees charged, or financial aid awarded—is more likely than ever before to get a quick and accurate reply from a polite and interested staff member to the degree that the law allows. The staff member is no longer frustrated at having to handle ton after ton of paper slips and handwritten forms. The parent receives the benefit of that changed attitude. The school as a whole takes on a much friendlier look.

Schools of higher education are already taking dramatic steps to connect their functioning *much* more closely with the job-market their students will face after graduating. At GW, for example, we pride ourselves on our internship and cooperative education programs, which help undergraduates to gain professional experience in their disciplines *while* they are still taking their classroom courses. And we're particularly proud, in this connection, of the good use we make of our community—the wonderful city of Washington, D.C., which so often looks like one enormous, throbbing heap of *opportunity*!

Are there any minuses to be added to this long list of pluses? Yes, there are—and it would be amazing, in an age as complex as our own, if this weren't the case. Higher education is at risk of losing a good deal of what used to be considered its relaxing charm—all of the images once associated with the "Halls of Ivy." We stand a risk, too, of losing the kinds of faculty members who might once have meditated for 20 years before producing a massive and definitive book. Students who want to explore freely and loosely—to do some intellectual wandering, in other words—may find everybody around them too intent on specialties, jobs and careers. *Serendipity*, once considered an academic virtue, may fall victim to productivity.

Those are risks we need to guard against, of course. But they're inevitable risks, and we will inevitably fall prey to at least some of them, in the new era of our bitterly competitive international economy. Today, those who produce goods and services have to work very hard indeed to convince their potential customers—potential customers in East Asia, Europe, Latin America, Australia, Africa and other places—that what they're selling is worth the price they're charging. And the exact same thing is true of our colleges and universities—even if most of their undergraduates still come from the 50 states of the Union. Whatever else they do in the future, schools of higher education will be prepared to justify the prices they charge to the students and families who *pay* those prices. To me, and I hope to you, that's good news!

THE BEGINNING OF WISDOM

My day job is being president of The George Washington University. However, I really start to work when I go home at night. There I am a *paterfamilias*. At home I am husband and father.

As I go about my job of being the father of two sons, I spend a great deal of my time thinking about equity. That's how you can tell I am the father. I think about "equity." My *sons*, especially when they were younger, called the same idea "fairness." Generational semantic differences may be amusing, but the meaning inside the words is no laughing matter—and, believe me, it never was.

If my wife and I brought home gifts for the boys, they had to be exactly the same. Even a different color was a legitimate cause for disputation between Adam and Ben. For a father, concerned with equity, this cut to the heart of the job. Or, speaking of cutting, what would happen when we had a cake for dessert?

One son could cut the cake, so son number two got the first lick of the cake knife—this time. Next time, I would have to remember who got first cut and who got first lick *last time*. And then, you know, not all licks are the same. Did the cake in question this time have a very thick butter-cream icing that stuck more plentifully to the cake-knife than the thinner chocolate icing of the last cake? Does first lick of the knife mean *both* sides of the blade? Was it the same knife—or was the knife we used last time larger?

I hasten to add that the particular intellectual constructs of equity or practical applications of fairness I used to solve the problem of cutting the cake were of no use at all when the question was the mixing bowl used for cookie dough, or who went down the slide in the playground first, or who got to answer the phone.

My sons are teenagers now. Cutting the cake or having identical blue water pistols are not problems any more. But fairness still is— even if, as young men now with their own views of the world, they

119

are beginning to think and talk about it as "equity." Even if their thoughts about equity are turning to what philosophers call "distributive justice." And even if they are genuinely concerned about how equity applies to others, not only themselves.

From this I conclude that my sons were paying more attention than their mother and father ever suspected. I also conclude that cutting the cake is a problem that never goes away: it's just that the cake doesn't look like a cake. It tends to look like the job market, or access to opportunity, or health care, or getting into the college of your choice, or something else—but always something. It looks like life.

I am thrilled that my sons are beginning to think in these terms— no more so than all your parents and relatives are thrilled with all of your growth and accomplishments which we are celebrating today. But as the floor show *du jour*, it presents me with a bit of a problem. Actually, two problems, and you could call both of them "telling the truth."

First, as you know, graduation speakers are supposed to talk about a commencement, not a graduation. As if "graduation," which comes from the Latin *gradus* meaning "step," is just too pale a word next to "commencement," which of course means "beginning." But if what I have been telling you about my own sons is true, and if the stories all your parents could tell on similar subjects are also true, then today is hardly the beginning of anything for you. In fact, it's the end of high school.

So, if I tell you that today you are commencing, you'll ask, "What? What am I commencing *today?*" And what am I supposed to say? Your life? If I say that, you'll find a way of reminding me—maybe even politely—that you've been alive for 17 or 18 years and ask, "So what was I doing up to now? Wasn't I learning to cut the cake? You mean going to Sidwell and dealing with my hormones and getting a driver's license wasn't living?"

Or maybe a nice young man—who happens to be one of you, graduating today—would tell me a little story about life and living. A couple of months ago, he thought it was time to line something up for his senior project. So he got on the phone and called an appropriately virtuous and utterly blameless social service agency. He introduced himself and said, "I have to do some community service." Without a moment's hesitation, the voice at the other end of the phone asked him, "Who's your probation officer?"

This nice young man from Sidwell Friends, this young man who was not yet 18 years old, learned that all of us are living in a society in which "community service" is a synonym for the soft alternative to doing hard time. It is *not*, in the minds of most people, our personal and voluntary effort to bring some measure of equity to an inequitable world: it's not the hard work of justice, but the easy way out of the criminal justice system. I'm more than three times his age, and I hadn't begun to learn that, or, you could say, I learned that from *his* life. And you all have your stories, too. So much for beginnings today.

That's just the first problem. If I abandon the routine flights of fancy on the theme of commencement and content myself—and you, too, I hope—with the step-taking notion of graduation, then I face the second problem of the speaker who wants to be truthful.

The standard and official version of the step-taking graduation speech tells you to "step out." Pick up the torch! Make the world better than the one your parents and I gave you! You may take three giant steps! Go forth! Be strong!

Of course, nearly all of you are going forth now, but mostly to a summer vacation or job and then to college. You will not be governing the nation, ending inequity or distributing world peace where it's needed most. Given my day job, I am very glad that you're going to college, and especially delighted that at least one of you has had the courtesy to have chosen to come to The George Washington University.

College will be very different from Sidwell Friends. It's my life's work to make sure it's different, but it's not your *life*. It's another step, and God willing it too will end with another step-taking ceremony, another graduation.

The step of college *may* be your defining moment. It was for me—or for part of my life. As an undergraduate at Columbia, I began asking what I was really good at. The answer was student government. That led to the question: so how do you make a living out of this?

The first part of the answer was simple: remain a student as long as you possibly can, and hope for a combination of understanding parents and generous grants. There followed a series of more difficult questions and answers which helped me shape my work life. But college may not be the defining moment for you. And remember, this was just one step leading to my day job I'm talking about: the way I earn my living, not my life.

A good step, as it turned out for me, but just one in my life. And not much different from the step my sons have already taken: cutting the cake has not been grounds for an argument between them for several years. But that is not to say that there are no longer any grounds for argument or any causes left for parental anxiety in our household. Adam and Ben have moved along to other agendas, with their mother and father following in their wake.

So, if what we are doing here today is not *the* beginning and if it's only one step of the many you are bound to take in the course of your lives, then why are we gathered here? It is a rite of passage—besides, every high school has a graduation. You would feel cheated without one.

And for good reason. Something has *been* happening to all of you during the last few years of your lives, and we need a ritual to mark it. This helps you to see what might otherwise remain invisible. All cultures do this with—or perhaps *to*—their young. Some go in for blood-letting and tattooing at the charismatic moment of passage. Others require different clothing or new haircuts, or carrying an emblem of adulthood, perhaps a weapon. We don't. We give you a piece of paper suitable for framing. Unless you are a bit odd and hang your diploma around your neck, it won't show when you walk down the street. No one will be able to tell, at a distance of a hundred paces, that you are now a full member of the clan or a certified defender of the faith or just old enough to come in out of the rain without being told. Our rites of passage mark something you can't see—and which I'll call the power to do well and good.

You have just finished up at the finest school in Washington. If your teachers have done their job, and you have done yours, then you have learned some useful and good things. Perhaps the best way to put it—and I regret to say that these apt words were first spoken by someone else—is that you have begun the lifelong process of "making the acquaintance of your own mind."

That, it seems to me, is something worth a ritual—with a pretty good party to follow. It means that you are on your way to puzzling out how to cut the many cakes that will be coming your way. It means that you possess both the power and the knowledge to *choose* to do good things, and to do them well—or to do otherwise. This, too, is no laughing matter, and it's something Mr. Vogel would want you to understand.

When I was in seventh grade, all the boys took what we used to call "shop." While the girls learned to sew and cook English muffin pizzas, the boys learned to distinguish a brad from a nail, male plugs from female, and other cultural artifacts presumed to be indispensable to a young man. I will not observe that this distinction according to gender is now considered antediluvian and illegal—and the wrong way to cut the cake.

Our shop teacher was Mr. Vogel, a lovely and humane person, an artisan and teacher, who loved sharing his craft with his students. I was a source of despair to Mr. Vogel because my bookends ended too soon or late, my tie racks were wracked or untied, and my lamps would not light. Nevertheless, I learned three useful and good things in Mr. Vogel's shop class.

First, I learned to respect a skilled worker. Second, I learned to avoid hammer, saw and, most especially, vice—of all kinds. And third, I learned what Mr. Vogel meant when I went to him with my current project in pieces, saying, "Look, Mr. Vogel, it broke."

Mr. Vogel would say, "Trachtenberg, it didn't break. *You* broke it."

Mr. Vogel was right: things don't break; we break them. The cake doesn't cut itself inequitably; we cut it. But if now you can break things or make the wrong cut, you have also arrived at the time of your life when you know how to fix things and cut straight and fairly.

This is the power you have now, and a very good reason to be here. We're celebrating your accomplishments and your acquisition of the intellectual tools of various trades. But it's more significant, I think, that we're celebrating the future successes of prosperity and equity that you have the power to make for yourselves and for others in your communities. Not just in your day jobs, but in your real work—in your lives.

ASSURING A GLOBAL PERSPECTIVE FOR THE AMERICAN COLLEGE STUDENT

In the world of business education, we have long witnessed a certain oscillation between what might be called "hard" and "soft" perspectives. At the "hard" end of the scale, there is typically an emphasis on quantifiable skills in areas involving finance. These skills enable the business executive to make tough but rapid decisions based on "the numbers."

But even in a time like our own, when there is so much emphasis on raising productivity by reducing the number of people on the payroll, the other end of the scale—the "soft" end—refuses to go away. As these radical cutbacks and restructurings proceed, voices are already being raised in alarm. Companies will suffer in the long run, these voices declare, if they don't pay attention to such less tangible issues as the morale of their employees, the internal need for continuity, and, above all, the corporate *culture*.

Even corporations have a culture! Such is one of the great discoveries of our age. Even corporations can benefit from the attention of social and behavioral scientists who once seemed limited to the study of distant tribes, of the urban poor, and of individual psychological problems. Companies that pay careful attention to their internal culture—to the unspoken assumptions and behavior patterns of their employees—will usually do better in the marketplace, even by "hard" standards, than those which assume that managers can make their decisions on the basis of finance alone.

If the world of business is currently incorporating an outlook of this kind, then how very attentive we must be in observing the assumptions and presuppositions represented by the cultures of different *nations*—especially since these can so strongly affect the roles those nations play in what we all now recognize as an *international* economy.

~~~~~~~~

~~~~~~~~

As my example for today, I give you the United States of America. By world standards, it is of course a very large country. And what that means in terms of daily experience is that an American can leave his or her home and travel for hundreds and thousands of miles, over a period of days or even weeks, without ever finding himself or herself in *another* country. Always the road signs are in English. Always the menus in the restaurants along the way are also in English. Always the newspapers being sold from machines outside those restaurants are English-language newspapers. And always the conversations taking place around the traveler are about Washington politics, or American football, baseball and basketball games, or the American television programs watched the night before.

If you stepped up to such a traveler and said: "Excuse me, but are you aware that you are having a cultural experience of a very particular kind?" then he or she would probably look quite surprised, and you might have to add: "You see, in most other parts of the world, people traveling as much as you're traveling right now might already have encountered five or six *different* languages and five or six *different* cultures. Why, in Western Europe, anyone who gets a job at a ski resort selling tickets for the ski-lift probably has to speak and understand French, English, German, Spanish and Italian—just for starters!"

Americans have trouble understanding that. When they travel abroad for pleasure, everybody around them seems to be able to speak English. When they go to a store that rents videocassettes, the most popular foreign movies have been *dubbed* into English—and even the less popular ones have English subtitles. When they watch the news on television, and a German official is addressing the Bundestag, there is *of course* a "voice-over" that translates his words into English. And when a Japanese businessman arrives in the United States to manage a factory or just to negotiate a single deal, the assumption is that he of course speaks fluent English, and that almost no American with whom he comes into contact can speak a word of Japanese.

Those from other countries who know these things about the culture of the United States may sometimes be surprised to discover that the teaching of foreign languages, to America's schoolchildren, is a major American industry. Starting in the high school years, and

~~~~~~~~

continuing on into the college years, every American boy and girl is required to spend *years* studying at least one foreign language—most often Spanish or French, occasionally German, and sometimes even Chinese or Japanese.

And yet, of all of these boys and girls, remarkably few ever achieve what, by international standards, would be regarded as true fluency in a language other than English. Meanwhile, large numbers of these young men and women regard their language classes as a "hassle" or a "bore" or a "waste of time."

Why is this the case? What is it that seems so missing in the American teaching and learning of foreign languages? And what must American educators do to restore this missing element? Those are the questions to which I would like to address my remarks.

Let me put my thoughts in a nutshell by saying that what American language study appears to lack is the sense of *urgency*. And let me, by way of contrast, refer to the *urgency* with which an American teenager, when applying for his or her first driver's license, *studies* the state-published booklets of laws and regulations that he or she must master in order to receive the license. In a matter of a few days, the teenager "has it all down pat." But after two or three years of studying Spanish or French, he or she might still be baffled if a question in French or Spanish isn't asked in the simplest possible way, as if one were addressing a five-year-old.

Now put yourself in the shoes of a French or German student studying English. Over the dinner-table, the student might hear a parent talking about a recent business trip through Holland, Belgium, Denmark and England. In Amsterdam, the parent encountered a businessman from right here in Japan, and they found it most comfortable to speak with each other in English. This led to the possibility of a piece of business that would significantly benefit the parent's company. And in England, where English was of course the language used in negotiation, the parent once again had to make some allowances for the difference between the British business culture and that of the "home country."

"I still have trouble getting used to it," the parent says across the dinner-table, "that way the British have of asking a question, in this rather offhand way, when what they're intending is to *make an important point*. Here in our own country, if the point is an important one, you lean forward, you speak in a firm way, and you probably tap a finger on the table. The British are always telling me how perfect my English is, but the language, all by itself, still isn't the *culture*."

And now I ask you: Is it any wonder that that student, hearing a parent talk in ways like these, makes a strong effort to acquire perfect English? And is it any wonder that most young people living in Holland or Germany or Denmark or Belgium today can speak helpfully to an American tourist, but that if they find themselves in New York or Washington or Chicago, they had better not count on someone speaking their own language helpfully to *them*?

In the United States, this problem has existed for so long that both Americans and those from other countries tend to take it for granted— as if it were a genetic defect. And yet we know that under conditions of sufficient urgency, Americans are capable of mastering the languages of other nations. Some of the most dramatic examples of this capability come, unfortunately, from the Second World War. Feeling themselves militarily threatened—feeling that their own survival and the survival of their nation were at stake—Americans in large numbers, and in an amazingly short time, were able to master the languages spoken and written by those who were then their adversaries.

It is a relief for me to be able to say that war—world war—is not the only example of this American capacity. Among Americans who have *already* succeeded in working their way up to important business positions, and who then are asked to engage in business dealings outside of the United States, this ability *also* makes itself felt. Indeed, there is now a rising *private* industry that involves teaching these business people a foreign language—enough of it to do business in—and to do so within a very short time.

The best-known of these companies is of course the one called Berlitz. But increasingly, as American business people have come to understand how little their foreign-language courses in high school and college have done for them, Berlitz has acquired a series of competitors. And to give you the flavor of what all of these companies are now doing, I would like to quote to you an article that appeared in an American newspaper, *The Hartford Courant*, on March 29th of this year:

"In just a week," the article began, "John Little zoomed through a Spanish textbook. Working on a rigorous eight-hour schedule for six consecutive days, Little also was able to put his new knowledge to use immediately: He had business dealings in Mexico the following week.

"Little . . . said he had no doubt about taking the intensive training . . . 'If you want to be effective, this is the thing to do.'

"Little—who studied at Inlingua School of Languages, the Switzerland-based language company that has an office in West Hartford—is an example of the growing number of business people seeking training in foreign languages.

"No longer willing to leave all of their communicating to translators, experts say Americans increasingly are seeing foreign languages and knowledge of other cultures as a competitive skill.

" 'My experience is that many business people who are thinking of international markets have misconceptions about how widespread English is, and how they will be perceived if they only speak English,' says Richard Shaw, a senior vice president for institutional investments for Phoenix Home Life Mutual Insurance Co.

"Over the years, Shaw has used Berlitz International and other classes to learn French and Italian for business.

"Shaw says his extensive world traveling has often brought him into contact with Americans who expect everyone to adapt to their limited language skills. In contrast, he says, he has found Japanese business people speaking German when they go to Germany."

I needn't quote any more of this article. You can see the dramatic moment that we have now reached in the history of American education. Only *outside* the school environment, it seems, are Americans able to generate the motivation—the sense of urgency—that makes it possible for them to master the languages, and to understand the cultures, of the other nations of the world.

And now let me pose the most difficult question of all, which is: Short of a world war, or some other sheer struggle for survival, how can Americans begin, at long last, to make a significant difference in this long-standing cultural pattern? Is it even conceivable that this could be accomplished?

Well, there is something of a revolution now underway in American education, one that may soon be making what is now *inconceivable* a lot more likely. It is the growing use of interactive video technology as a teaching tool in both our high schools and our colleges. At Washington State University, for example, $25 million has been spent over the last four years to develop a "multimedia center" that enables teachers to call up, at the push of a button, all kinds of computerized materials that they want their students to see and to hear in the lecture room. Eventually, Washington State hopes that each and every student, using a computer in his or her dormitory room, will be able to call up these same materials for review purposes—for example, when preparing for examinations. The entire campus is being rewired with fiber-optic cable in order to make this intensively computerized learning environment possible.

But the key word is *interactive*. Using technology of this kind in an *interactive* manner, teachers and their students, seated in the classroom, can make *live* contact with practically any part of the world. Indeed, one American high school class has already been meeting, on a weekly basis, with a group of similar students in Finland.

You can see the possibilities that this kind of technology opens— *especially* when it comes to matters of language and culture. One of the lessons of our century has been that people learn languages most quickly in some kind of *immersion* situation, such as visiting a foreign country, staying with a family there, and having almost no opportunity to speak their *own* language. The problem has always been how to make this kind of immersion experience possible at lower expense.

The problem has also been how to achieve a similar sense of *urgency*—of sheer *incentive to learn*—when the student is *here* rather than *there*. If an American knows that in an hour or two, he or she is going to be sitting at the dinner-table with a French family whose members speak no English, then there is an obvious incentive to avoid being embarrassed—to speak French as grammatically and fluently as possible. How can this be achieved without an expensive trip abroad?

Now imagine that you are an American student who, via interactive television and satellite technology, will soon be having a conversation with a group of French students who have been cautioned *not* to slip into English, no matter how desperate their American interlocutors may become.   Or suppose you are an American student who will soon be using the same technology to ask questions of a member of the French government? Presto! The incentive—the *urgency*—has been made part of the picture.

But there is yet another aspect of contemporary information technology that can help students to achieve an appropriate immersion in another culture and another linguistic mode. It is what is usually referred to as *virtual reality*, and it's often used, these days, to train airplane pilots or other highly technologized personnel by enveloping them—via special helmets and suits—in a *simulated* reality that closely resembles the one they must master. The trainee hears an alarm go off. The trainee, on the simulated radar screen, sees all the signs of another plane approaching on a collision course. The trainee must do all of the things that a real pilot would do in order to avoid the disaster. Meanwhile, the computer program that controls the process is capable of sending up all kinds of unexpected challenges that require this or that form of detailed response.

You can see the obvious ways in which this technology can be adapted for teaching purposes, and probably at considerably lower expense. The student can be plunged into the simulated reality of a French railway station. The situation can be made as dramatic as one wishes. A terrorist attack has taken place. The station is littered with debris. A French policeman rushes up to the student and starts to ask, in French, the appropriate questions: "Who are you? What are you doing here? Where are you going? Did you see anyone running past you?" And afterwards, when the recording is played on the big screen in front of the room, the entire class can join in critiquing the student's responses.

I describe a "world of the future." But I describe that world using a technology that is *already* at our fingertips. And the question now is: Can the *resources* be made available—the *money*—and can the will be generated, to transform the American study of what are called, from the American point of view, "foreign" languages and "foreign" cultures?

One thing is certain: Americans, like all the other peoples of the world, are having to cope with a truly globalized economy. Compared to many other nations, including almost all the major industrial powers, their ability to cope with this new world is being hampered by certain traditional handicaps. Average Americans are spending *years* of study in foreign languages, with little discernible effect. Only far-*above*-average Americans—those who rise high enough in a business organization—are then given the opportunity to *redo* their educations and to finally learn what they should have learned long before.

This is not a healthy situation. It is not good for the American economy. And it is not good for American foreign policy, either, which needs an informed electorate in order to function effectively, as well as State Department personnel who are deeply versed in the ways of other cultures and societies.

When hearing proposals like those I have made today, the first impulse of many Americans will be to cry: "They're far too expensive! The technology alone would cost a *fortune* to install!" Only when the alternatives are carefully considered—the alternatives involved in continuing the present counterproductive system of teaching other languages and other cultures—only then will the costs seem perfectly reasonable.

THE IMPORTANCE OF ANCIENT HISTORY

Thirty-eight years ago, when the world was young, I sat where you are sitting now—together with the other members of the Class of 1959—and listened to Dean Nicholas McKnight while he tried to electrify us with the importance of our Columbia education.

And when Dean McKnight pointed his forefinger in our general direction, and declared that sitting among us there might very well be a future winner of the Nobel Prize, I was personally electrified.

Would that brilliant and world-famous individual turn out to be none other than ME? Should I dedicate myself and my resources wholeheartedly to achieving that Swedish pinnacle of triumph?

As I made my way from Columbia College through the various stages of my career, therefore, I actually experienced mad, immodest moments when McKnight's words came crowding inadvertently back into my mind. I'd stand there in front of the bathroom mirror, making faces at myself, with shaving cream on my cheeks, and I'd ask myself: "Does what I'm doing with my life right now make it more or less likely that the King of Sweden will one day be draping the Nobel Prize around my neck, and passing me a very generous check in addition?"

And then it happened. To my delight, my fellow member of the Class of '59, Professor Roald Hoffmann, now of Cornell University, won the Nobel Prize for Chemistry.

Roald is a modern-style chemist and a poet. He does his work not in a laboratory with test-tubes and beakers and bunsen-burners but in an office, with computers. And when the announcement about his Nobel Prize came through in the media, I sent him a letter of rejoicing, just so he'd have some idea of the weight he had lifted off my weary, unworthy shoulders. Rather than be chasing so unlikely a possibility as the Nobel Prize, I could finally settle down to the calm, placid and dignified life of a university president—someone whose only day-to-day worries, as President Rupp can testify, focus on modest matters of institutional finance, legal actions, curricular upheaval, faculty disputations, journalistic and political denunciations, and the occasional student excesses.

But now, as I get ready to say a few words to you—words that, if they perhaps stay with you at all beyond tomorrow's lunch, hopefully won't do so in quite as compulsive a way as those that Dean McKnight spoke in 1955—I find myself filled with what one might call chronological doubt.

If this were 1965, I'd tell you what a great contemplative place Columbia College is—and not to feel too anxious about the recent demonstrations on campus, including the riotous occupation of President Kirk's office, because the measure of a Columbia education cannot be impacted by such transient historical eruptions.

And if this were 1975, then I'd tell you what a great contemplative place Columbia College is—and not to feel too anxious about the runaway inflation currently impacting on our national economy, because the value of a Columbia education even has a material aspect. Those whose minds have been sharpened here will be able to carve a successful career for themselves even in a 1975 America where mortgage rates are moving toward 16 percent.

If this were 1985, on the other hand, I'd tell you what a great contemplative place Columbia College is—and not to be swept away by the excessive quest for wealth that has become the hallmark of the Reagan Years. A Columbia education, I would labor to prove, enables one to rise above such Niagaras of mass enthusiasm as the love of cash and the lust for expensive goodies that is currently animating the American Zeitgeist.

But this is neither 1955 nor 1965 nor 1975 nor 1985. This is 1993—a time of fingernail-chomping worry about jobs and careers and the international economy—a time when, we're told, the levels of competition for which we need to prepare ourselves are streaking through the ionosphere on their way to outer space, and the question I'm asking myself therefore runs as follows: "Once I get through telling them what a great contemplative place Columbia College is, and how much I enjoyed my four years here on *Spectator* and Student Board and how later my Columbia education—both on campus and at the West End—helped me at every point in my own personal and professional life, then what else can I say to them in a time as frequently scary and dismaying as the present?" Without growing sentimental, it is fair to note that what happens between today and commencement is likely to have an impact on your development. The campus, the teachers, the city all create a special experience that forms Columbia men and women. And you can always tell Columbia men and women, but you can't tell them much.

A few words of counsel: What you need to be during your years as a Columbia student, and your subsequent years as a Columbia graduate, is ruthless, suspicious and utterly devoid of compromise.

Be ruthless with yourself. Just because one of your instructors likes the work you've done is no reason to rest content. Maybe he or she was just having a good day, and it carried over into his or her grading. Keep your personal, intellectual and ethical standards even higher than those of your teachers and bosses, and you can't go wrong.

Be morbidly suspicious of everything you're told—particularly at events like this by people like me who may reflect too uncritically on the Columbia they knew as undergraduates—and of everything you read. In a world that plays as fast and loose with evidence as the one we're living in right now, a world in which seeing is not believing, Columbia's traditional emphasis on primary as opposed to secondary sources has a very special importance.

But even at Columbia, teachers have to rely, sometimes, on information from secondary sources. In the Humanities sequence, for example, major works of literature written in languages other than English are studied and discussed in translation. And when a student is able to demonstrate that the original source contradicts its English version—that the original Greek or Hebrew or Sanskrit or Chinese has been incorrectly translated—then a truly fine teacher, the kind of teacher you're very likely to encounter at Columbia, breaks into spontaneous applause.

Finally, I suggest that you be utterly devoid of compromise—at least where intellectual matters are concerned. Don't let the historical phenomenon called fanaticism give dedication a bad name. Never

ever change your mind unless someone gives you an excellent reason for doing so. Be critical and ask hard questions that go right to the core, even if that core has been venerated by generations of prior Columbia students.

Having given you these pieces of good advice, so in harmony with the spirit of the difficult age in which we live, I'd like to conclude by urging you—as you practice this high degree of ruthlessness, suspiciousness and utter refusal to compromise—not to forget the virtue known as compassion. And just to make sure you don't forget it, I'm going to exercise it in front of your very eyes.

Seated in your midst is a brand new Columbia freshman whose last name is the same as my own and whose first name is Adam. He's been listening to me for more than 18 years now—at the breakfast table, over lunch, at dinnertime, and under other circumstances as well. Finally he gets away from home. Finally he comes all the way to New York and to Morningside Heights. And what should he hear once he gets here but that old familiar voice. I feel flooded with compassion for Adam when I think of it. I hope you are, too.

I know that with your contribution, Columbia College will move forward from strength to strength, remaining a place of joy, a place where the standard of excellence is tempered with civility, decency and humanity. And I'll conclude these remarks by saying that I've looked at every one of you in the course of making them, and that you all—each and every one of you—look like Nobel Prize winners to me!

AFTERWORD

The words of E.B. White came to mind during my reading of Steve Trachtenberg's delightfully wise, provocative, and enterprising essays. White once wrote that he "awoke each morning determined both to change the world and to have one heluva good time. Sometimes," he went on to say, "that made planning the day a little difficult." Steve seems to be having one heluva good time and certainly, from his bully pulpit, as president of one of our best universities, is also attempting to change the way we think about the modern university. That's a tall order, what is sometimes called in the trade a paradigm shift, a fancy phrase which basically means "the way we look at things." Any reader of this book, I promise you, will change the way they look at our institutions of "the higher learning."

As a former university president myself, I marvel at Steve's capacity to wonder aloud with such elegant ruminations, fearlessly challenging a lot of sacred cows and canons, always with a sense of humor, balance, common sense, and without rancor or hubris. While he is sometimes at an angle to the conventional wisdom of academia, he invites us into a dialogue with him with such brio and humor that I doubt that **anyone** would be immune to his arguments. Reading his essays is a very personal experience, sort of like sitting around a campfire and exchanging ideas which keep us warm.

In one of my favorite essays, Steve confronts the major challenges facing universities today: high tuition, scandals over intercollegiate athletics, multi-culturalism, "political correctness," media overkill, quotas, tenure, faculty productivity, conflicting missions, and lots more. He doesn't mince words and his face is always windward and without that omega look of so many of his colleagues who tend to emphasize the "worst of times." Steve, withal, always manages to notice the "best of times" as well, even in this age of redefinition and change. I'll never forget Bart Giamatti's lapidary phrase about the life of a university president: "Being president of a university is no way for an adult to make a living." After reading these essays, I have to agree. But it's clear to me that Steve isn't a university president to "make a living"; he's in it, knowing he's playing for mortal stakes and because he seems to be having one heluva good time.

Quoting some unnamed source with obvious agreement, Steve argues that education is "making the acquaintance of your own mind." Seems to me that's what Steve does in these essays, acquainting himself with his own ideas and points of view.

I guess what most impressed me about this book is that Steve does his own thinking and writing, like very, very few of his colleagues do. He comes out of the tradition of great university presidents. Giants like Hutchins, Butler, and Kerr come to mind, people who not only made history but wrote about it. Those leaders who increasingly rely on their staffs to do their thinking for them become incapacitated to do precisely what's so vital in leadership: **thinking**. Thinking about the purposes and tactics, about technologies and the people they need to take on and educate. In this hazardous age of fast change, it is especially important that leaders think carefully for themselves. Because, in the words of Robert Graves:

Experts ranked in serried rows
Filled the enormous plaza full.
*But only one there who **knows***
And he's the man who fights the bull.

The people who fight the bull (no pun intended) do not live in the breezy world that journalists dream up — and certainly not the world of the critics in the bleachers. The successful leader which Stephen Joel Trachtenberg exemplifies fights the bull and lives, Janus-like, in the world of ideas and the world of business. It's a world that requires real work, and it doesn't get done with rhetoric or shortcuts or group think. Steve does it with panache, humor, and a big, broad intelligence. —*Warren Bennis*

Warren Bennis is University Professor and Distinguished Professor of Business Administration at the University of Southern California.